Options	Page	Type
√ Rulers		^R
√ Snap to rulers		Sh^Y
Zero lock		
√ Guides		^J
√ Snap to guides		^U
√ Lock guides		
Column guides...		
Autoflow		
Index entry...		^;
Show index...		
Create index...		
Create TOC...		

Page	Type	Element
√ Fit in window		^W
25% size		^0
50% size		^5
75% size		^7
Actual size		^1
200% size		^2
400% size		^4
Go to page...		^G
Insert pages...		
Remove pages...		
√ Display master items		
Copy master guides		

Look for the *Up & Running* books on a variety of popular software and hardware topics. Current titles include:

Up & Running with AutoSketch

Up & Running with Carbon Copy Plus

Up & Running with DOS 3.3

Up & Running with Flight Simulator

Up & Running with Harvard Graphics

Up & Running with Lotus 1-2-3 Release 2.2

Up & Running with Norton Utilities

Up & Running with PageMaker on the Macintosh

Up & Running with PC Tools Deluxe 6

Up & Running with PC-Write

Up & Running with PROCOMM PLUS

Up & Running with Q & A

Up & Running with Quattro Pro 2

Up & Running with Turbo Pascal 5.5

Up & Running with Windows 3.0

Up & Running with Windows 286/386

Up & Running with WordPerfect Library/Office PC

Up & Running with Your Hard Disk

Computer users are not all alike.
Neither are SYBEX books.

We know our customers have a variety of needs. They've told us so. And because we've listened, we've developed several distinct types of books to meet the needs of each of our customers. What are you looking for in computer help?

If you're looking for the basics, try the **ABC's** series. You'll find short, unintimidating tutorials and helpful illustrations. For a more visual approach, select **Teach Yourself**, featuring screen-by-screen illustrations of how to use your latest software purchase.

Mastering and **Understanding** titles offer you a step-by-step introduction, plus an in-depth examination of intermediate-level features, to use as you progress.

Our **Up & Running** series is designed for computer-literate consumers who want a no-nonsense overview of new programs. Just 20 basic lessons, and you're on your way.

We also publish two types of reference books. Our **Instant References** provide quick access to each of a program's commands and functions. SYBEX **Encyclopedias** provide a *comprehensive reference* and explanation of all of the commands, features and functions of the subject software.

Sometimes a subject requires a special treatment that our standard series doesn't provide. So you'll find we have titles like **Advanced Techniques, Handbooks, Tips & Tricks**, and others that are specifically tailored to satisfy a unique need.

We carefully select our authors for their in-depth understanding of the software they're writing about, as well as their ability to write clearly and communicate effectively. Each manuscript is thoroughly reviewed by our technical staff to ensure its complete accuracy. Our production department makes sure it's easy to use. All of this adds up to the highest quality books available, consistently appearing on best seller charts worldwide.

You'll find SYBEX publishes a variety of books on every popular software package. Looking for computer help? Help Yourself to SYBEX.

For a complete catalog of our publications:

SYBEX Inc.

2021 Challenger Drive, Alameda, CA 94501

Tel: (415) 523-8233/(800) 227-2346 Telex: 336311

SYBEX   Fax: (415) 523-2373

Up & Running with
PageMaker® 4 on the PC

Marvin Bryan

SYBEX®

San Francisco • Paris • Düsseldorf • Soest

Acquisitions Editor: David J. Clark
Series Editor: Joanne Cuthbertson
Editor: Kathleen Lattinville
Technical Editor: Nick Dargahi
Word Processors: Paul Erickson, Deborah Maizels
Book Designer: Elke Hermanowski
Icon Designer: Helen Bruno
Screen Graphics: Cuong Le
Desktop Production Artist: Eleanor Ramos
Proofreaders: Lisa Haden, Hilda Van Genderen
Indexer: Nancy Alderman Guenther
Cover Designer: Archer Design
Screen reproductions produced by XenoFont.

Library of Congress Card Number: 90-71936
ISBN: 0-89588-781-9

Manufactured in the United States of America
10 9 8 7 6 5 4 3 2 1

SYBEX
Up & Running Books

The Up & Running series of books from SYBEX has been developed for committed, eager PC users who would like to become familiar with a wide variety of programs and operations as quickly as possible. We assume that you are comfortable with your PC and that you know the basic functions of word processing, spreadsheets, and database management. With this background, Up & Running books will show you in 20 steps what particular products can do and how to use them.

Who this book is for

Up & Running books are designed to save you time and money. First, you can avoid purchase mistakes by previewing products before you buy them—exploring their features, strengths, and limitations. Second, once you decide to purchase a product, you can learn its basics quickly by following the 20 steps—even if you are a beginner.

What this book provides

The first step usually covers software installation in relation to hardware requirements. You'll learn whether the program can operate with your available hardware as well as various methods for starting the program. The second step often introduces the program's user interface. The remaining 18 steps demonstrate the program's basic functions, using examples and short descriptions.

Contents and structure

 A clock shows the amount of time you can expect to spend at your computer for each step. Naturally, you'll need much less time if you only read through the step rather than complete it at your computer.

Special symbols and notes

You can also focus on particular points by scanning the short notes in the margins and locating the sections you are most interested in.

In addition, three symbols highlight particular sections of text:

- The Action symbol highlights important steps that you will carry out.

- The Tip symbol indicates a practical hint or special technique.

- The Warning symbol alerts you to a potential problem and suggestions for avoiding it.

We have structured the Up & Running books so that the busy user spends little time studying documentation and is not burdened with unnecessary text. An Up & Running book cannot, of course, replace a lengthier book that contains advanced applications. However, you will get the information you need to put the program to practical use and to learn its basic functions in the shortest possible time.

We
welcome
your
comments

SYBEX is very interested in your reactions to the Up & Running series. Your opinions and suggestions will help all of our readers, including yourself. Please send your comments to: SYBEX Editorial Department, 2021 Challenger Drive, Alameda, CA 94501.

Preface

You're about to get acquainted with a very powerful resource: Aldus PageMaker 4.0 on the PC—the latest version of a classic desktop publishing program. PageMaker runs in the Windows operating environment, which has also been enhanced with new powers recently. The combination is hard to beat.

Although PageMaker has many capabilities, they're easier to use than ever. This book will have you "up and running" in no time.

What is desktop publishing? As the term implies, it's the process of creating publications on your own desktop. You can also print them from your desktop if you have an appropriate printer, or you can make files to take to a professional printshop that will do the actual printing for you. Your publications may be one-page announcements, multipage newsletters, training manuals, or full-length books of any kind—you're only limited by your own imagination.

With the current version of PageMaker, you can start the publication process right inside the program itself, using the *Story editor* — actually a mini word-processor that's one of the recently added features. Here you can write your document and even check its spelling. Of course, you can also import documents created with word-processing programs such as Microsoft Word, WordPerfect, or WordStar.

In addition, you can import graphics, spreadsheets, and database records, and combine them all in sharp-looking documents.

In PageMaker it's a snap to set up *master pages* that establish where the major elements of your pages will be located—the margins, columns, headings, and graphic elements. Then you can quickly perform such tricks as flowing text from column to column, placing and sizing illustrations exactly as you want them, and making shaded boxes to hold information you want given special attention.

You can make *templates* and *style sheets* so you can create a series of publications (such as a monthly report) with a uniform layout and general appearance. You can add and use a variety of typefaces, setting up your documents so that specific fonts will be selected automatically for subheadings or captions. For most printers, you can now create fonts automatically *on the fly* in any size for both the printer and the screen. This means the fonts are built as you need them; no longer is it necessary to store fonts on your hard disk in a variety of fixed sizes.

All of these subjects and more are explained in this book— covered in 20 easy Steps. If you're new to PageMaker or to the latest version, you can become productive in a hurry. If you haven't bought the program yet, this review of its features can help you make an informed decision.

—Marvin Bryan

Table of Contents

Step 1
Installing PageMaker

Installing PageMaker is simple. The process consists primarily of following on-screen prompts that ask you questions about your equipment and which features of the program you want to install. The software then performs the actual installation automatically. However, you do need to know in advance what software and hardware are required to use PageMaker. You'll also need to know a few details about the questions PageMaker asks so you can give the correct answers. This Step provides you with this information.

What You'll Need

PageMaker 4.0 runs only under Windows 3.0 (or a later version). In the past, many software developers would sell a product running under Windows in a package that included a *runtime* version of Windows itself—that is, a special version of Windows that would function only with that product. There are no runtime versions of Windows 3.0. You must buy and install a full version of Windows 3.0 before you install PageMaker.

Windows is a graphic-based work environment that uses version 3.1 or later of the MS-DOS operating system. Although Windows will run on a computer such as an IBM PC with an Intel 8086 or 8088 processor (but not well), PageMaker and most other applications written for Windows require more powerful computers using an 80286, 80386, or 80486 processor. PageMaker also requires a hard disk with at least 5 megabytes (MB)—preferably, 6MB—of free disk space to install the complete package. You will also need 2MB—preferably, 3MB—of random-access memory (RAM), a Microsoft-compatible mouse, and at least an EGA monitor (VGA is preferred). You can use any printer compatible with Windows 3.0. In order to use the disks furnished for installation, you must have either a 3½" (720K or 1.4MB) floppy drive or a 5¼" high-density (1.2MB) floppy drive.

Many computer systems sold today fulfill these requirements or can be upgraded to comply with them.

Starting the Installation

Follow this procedure to begin the PageMaker installation:

1. Install Windows 3.0, following the directions in the Windows manual.

2. Make working copies of your original PageMaker disks, using the DOS command **DISKCOPY**. (See your DOS manual if you're unsure of the procedure.)

3. Place the working copy of the PageMaker Disk 1 into drive A. (If your floppy drive is labeled B, substitute *B* for *A* in these instructions.)

4. Start Windows and open the **Windows Program Manager**.

5. Pull down the **File** menu and choose the **Run...** command, as shown in Figure 1.1. (The three dots after the word Run are called an *ellipsis*. Usually, a command followed by an ellipsis is not executed the instant you select it; instead, selecting the command causes a *dialog box* to appear, requiring you to make some choice or provide additional information. In this case, the **Run** dialog box will appear.)

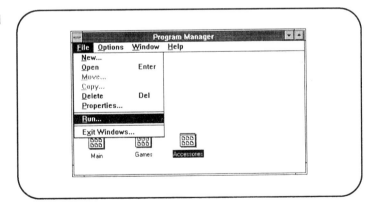

Figure 1.1: Selecting the Run... Command in the Windows Program Manager

6. On the **Command Line** of the **Run** dialog box, type the following: **A:ALDSETUP** (see Figure 1.2). Then click **OK**. (If your floppy drive is B, type **B:ALDSETUP**.) The **Aldus Setup** Main Window will appear, and then a **Select directory** dialog box that will propose **C:\ALDUS** as the directory for Aldus files. Click **OK** to accept this, or type in another location for the files, and then click **OK**. The setup window will reappear, now listing options available for installation. In this window, you select the options you want installed by highlighting them (see Figure 1.3).

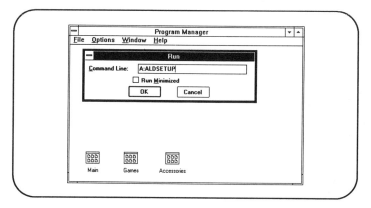

Figure 1.2: Entering the command to run Aldus Setup

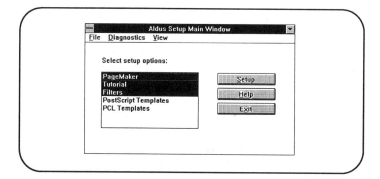

Figure 1.3: Setup installation options

Selecting Setup Options

The exact options you will see in the **Aldus Setup** window will depend upon the exact version of PageMaker you're using. However, the following options will probably be displayed:

- **PageMaker**. This option installs the PageMaker program, the Table editor, the Setup program (so you can make installation changes later to handle circumstances such as the purchase of a new printer), Help and Readme files, the spellchecker, and a hyphenation dictionary. Obviously, you must have this option selected because it includes files required to run PageMaker.

- **Tutorial**. If you're already familiar with other versions of PageMaker and feel you can learn the new features by reading and experimentation, you could skip the tutorial files. If you have plenty of disk space, you may want to install them anyway, just in case you run into a problem or someone else wants to learn the program on your computer.

- **Filters**. Filters are used to exchange text and graphic files with other applications by converting file formats. If you don't select this option, you can't do any importing and exporting. However, you don't have to install all of the filters that PageMaker provides. When you select this option, you'll see all of the filters displayed during the installation process. You can choose only the ones you know you'll need. For example, if you don't plan to export PageMaker files and will always import text from WordStar and graphics in the .PCX format, selecting just those filters will save a lot of disk space. You can always run **Aldus Setup** again to add more filters.

- **PostScript Templates**. If you have a PostScript printer, select this option to have sample templates installed. These templates provide complete models (with layout, type sizes, etc.) for producing flyers, newsletters, brochures, price lists, and other common types of publications. You can customize and change the templates so you can insert your own text, graphics, typefaces, and so on. These templates can save you time and give you ideas for your own layouts. You will be given the opportunity to select the individual templates you want installed.

- **PCL Templates.** If you have a printer in the Hewlett-Packard LaserJet family or some other printer that can use that company's Printer Command Language (PCL), select this option to install the PCL equivalents of the PostScript templates described in the preceding paragraph.

To select or deselect individual Setup options, press the **Ctrl** key as you click the left mouse button. To select a *range* of options, click the first option, and then hold down the **Shift** key as you click the last option in the range.

When you're finished, click the **Setup** button. Now you'll see a **Select directory** dialog box again.

Later, when you're asked to make specific filter and template selections in the **Aldus Setup** window, the installation program will keep track of the amount of space you'll need for each option. At the bottom of the screen you'll see a changing display indicating how much room remains on your hard disk. You'll be warned if a selection will require more disk space than is available.

If you need more disk storage than is available, a number will be displayed at the bottom of the screen preceded by a minus sign. This figure represents how much more space you need.

You can free that extra disk space without leaving **Aldus Setup**. Remember, Windows 3.0 lets you run more than one application at a time. Simply call up the **Windows File Manager** and delete files you don't need from your disk. Then return to the **Aldus Setup** window and continue with the installation.

Here are the detailed instructions:

1. Double-click the **Program Manager** icon to open the **Program Manager** window.

2. From the **Program Manager** window, double-click the **Main** icon to open the **Main** window.

3. From the **Main** window, double-click the **File Manager** icon to open the **File Manager** window.

4. Click disk and/or directory icons and use the horizontal scroll bar as necessary to display files you want to delete.

5. Click to highlight a file you want to delete; its size in bytes will be displayed at the bottom of the window. Press the **Del** key to delete the file. (If you wish to delete more than one displayed file, select multiple files by holding down the **Ctrl** key as you click on them, and then pressing **Del**. To delete a series of sequential files, click to select the first file, hold down the **Shift** key, and select the last file in the sequence; the clicked files will be highlighted, as well as all of those in between. Press **Del** to delete them all.)

6. The **Delete** dialog box will appear. The names of the file(s) selected for deletion will be displayed. Click the **Delete** button.

7. A **File Manager** warning box will appear, displaying one file name at a time. Click **Yes** to confirm the deletion of each one.

8. Close the **File Manager** and return to **Aldus Setup**.

When you've completed your selection of options to install, click the **Setup** box or press **S** to proceed.

Completing the Installation

The remainder of the installation is almost automatic, unless (as explained earlier) you have to leave the **Aldus Setup** window temporarily to free more disk space. Here's the procedure:

1. **Aldus Setup** will ask you for the drive and directory where you want PageMaker installed. Accept **C:\PM4** (the default), or type any other DOS path and directory name you like. You can select any other available drive on your system, provided it has adequate room to store the files. Click **OK** when you've finished.

2. Next "personalize your product" by typing your name, company name, and PageMaker serial number in the dialog box that appears. This information will be displayed each time the program is loaded.

3. You'll be asked if you want **Setup** to make necessary modifications to your AUTOEXEC.BAT and CONFIG.SYS files. If you answer **Yes**, the program will make sure that CONFIG.SYS contains the statements **FILES=20** and **BUFFERS=30**. Existing higher numbers will be allowed to remain for the FILES and BUFFERS statements if they are there. Your PageMaker directory will be added to the **PATH** statement in your AUTOEXEC.BAT file. A **SET TEMP** statement listing that directory will also be added (example: **SET TEMP=C:\PM**). If you don't want the program to make these modifications, you'll have to do them yourself, either with the Windows Notepad accessory or a word processor that can produce ASCII files. If you answer **No**, to make the changes yourself, you can specify some other directory for temporary files (example: **SET TEMP=D:\TEMP**).

4. Select the file import/export filters you want from the list that appears (unless you did not select **Filters** for installation). Remember, you can run **Aldus Setup** again if you want to add more later. Click **OK** when you're finished.

5. Select the templates you want copied to your hard disk from the lists that will appear if you've chosen to install templates. You can add others later by running **Aldus Setup** again. Click **OK** when you're finished.

Setup will ask you to insert various disks as it needs them. When installation is complete, you will see a notice stating that the items you selected have been successfully installed; click **OK,** and then **Exit.** You must reboot your computer so that changes made can take effect.

PageMaker files are in compressed form on the disks provided. You cannot install the program by merely copying their contents into a directory on your hard disk. You must use the **Aldus Setup** installation program so the files will be expanded into a usable condition.

Step 2
Adding Typefaces

Although many users of word-processing programs get along very nicely by printing all of their documents in the Courier typeface (which resembles the output of a typewriter), using a variety of typefaces is almost an essential for desktop-publishing operations. With PageMaker you can use any typeface already installed in your copy of Windows 3.0, and you can purchase many more from vendors. Most of these vendors also have installation programs that will install the typefaces into Windows automatically.

If you haven't used typefaces extensively in the past, you may find the following definitions useful:

- *Font.* Typefaces are sometimes referred to as *fonts.* However, strictly speaking, a font is a particular typeface in a specific size with specific style attributes. For example, *Times Roman 10 pt. bold* is one font; *Times Roman 10 pt. italic* is a different font—but they are both members of the Times Roman typeface family.

- *Typeface.* A group of fonts with common identifiable design characteristics.

- *Point.* (abbreviated *pt.*) A measurement standard used for typefaces in the printing and publishing industries. A point is approximately 1/72 of an inch.

PageMaker supports the use of fonts from 4 pt. to 650 pt. in size. (One 650 pt. character can fill an entire page.) You can create both screen and printer fonts in any of these sizes you specify in your documents, if you have the Windows version of Adobe Type Manager (ATM). Fortunately, ATM is included with each copy of PageMaker 4.0. ATM uses typeface *outlines,* which are actually computer routines that mathematically generate and scale characters on demand. Outlines for several typeface styles are included in the ATM package, which will be explained later in this Step.

However, if you have previous experience with desktop publishing or word processing on IBM-compatible computers, you have probably already purchased other typeface packages. The first section will tell you how you can make use of them in PageMaker.

Using Typefaces You Already Have

The fonts you want to add to Windows for use in PageMaker may already be stored in a directory on your hard disk. Windows can access fonts stored on floppy disks; however, if you leave fonts on floppies, you have to remember to insert the correct floppy into a drive every time you want to use them. So, if you have enough hard-disk space, it's strongly recommended that you transfer your fonts to your hard disk.

You can install most existing typefaces with tools provided within Windows itself. You access these utilities through the Windows **Control Panel**, shown in Figure 2.1. The Windows utilities will also copy the files for you.

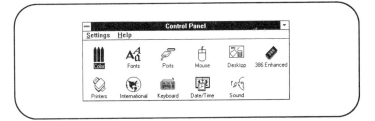

Figure 2.1: The Control Panel window

Here's how to access the **Control Panel:**

1. Double-click the **Program Manager** icon to open the **Program Manager** window.

2. From the **Program Manager** window, double-click the **Main** icon to open the **Main** window.

3. From the **Main** window, double-click the **Control Panel** icon to open the **Control Panel** window.

Installing Screen Fonts

When you install Windows, a few typefaces are automatically installed. Some are *raster* (or *bitmapped*) fonts; these are fonts that come in fixed sizes, composed of patterns of tiny dots. The program's "Helv" raster fonts (a version of the Helvetica type style) are used to create the Windows screens, including menus.

The other built-in typefaces are *vector*—meaning that they can be scaled on demand to different sizes.

If you have no other fonts installed, these built-in typefaces will be used for printing. They will also be used for creating approximations of your typefaces for screen fonts, in case you have no screen fonts for the typefaces you've specified.

If you want to install additional screen fonts into Windows, follow this procedure:

1. Insert the disk containing the fonts into a floppy drive if they are not already on your hard drive.

2. Display the **Control Panel** window and click the **Fonts** icon. You will see the **Fonts** dialog box, shown in (Figure 2.2). The list box will display the names of typefaces for which screen fonts are already installed. By highlighting a name on the list, you can see samples of the fonts.

3. Click the **Add...** button. The **Add Font Files** dialog box will appear (see Figure 2.3). The names of the screen font files in the current directory will be displayed in the left list box. Other directories and drives from which you can choose will be shown in the **Directories** list box on the right.

4. If you know the name and path for a screen font you want to install into Windows, you can type this information in the **Font Filename** text box at the top of the dialog box.

5. If you're unsure of the exact font name or if you want to install several fonts from another directory on hard disk, select a new drive and/or directory from the **Directories**

list box. To add fonts from a floppy disk, select the appropriate floppy drive.

6. Click a font name to highlight and select it. Select as many as you like. If you change your mind about adding a specific font, click its name again to deselect it.

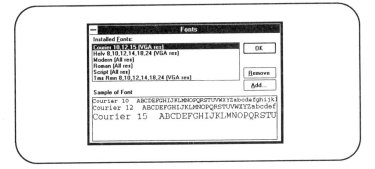

Figure 2.2: The Fonts dialog box

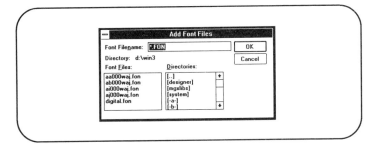

Figure 2.3: The Add Font Files dialog box

7. Click **OK** to add the font(s).

Installing Printer Fonts

Printer fonts cannot be installed through the **Fonts** dialog box. You must click the **Printers** icon and work your way through a series of submenus. This option installs bitmapped fonts, which cannot be used by a PostScript printer. Therefore, the following font-installation information applies only to non-PostScript printers. Here are the details:

1. If you'll be adding fonts not already stored on your hard drive, insert the disk containing the fonts into a floppy drive.

2. Display the **Control Panel** window and double-click the **Printers** icon. You'll see the **Printers** dialog box.

3. Click the **Configure...** button. You'll see the **Printers-Configure** dialog box.

4. Click the **Setup...** button. In the **Setup** dialog box, you can change the selected printer (from those supported by the current printer driver) and specify the paper source, size, and orientation; the graphics resolution; number of copies; and other options.

5. Click the **Fonts...** button. Finally, you'll see the **Printer Font Installer** dialog box. If you haven't installed any printer fonts into Windows yet, the left-hand list box will display a message reading: *No fonts installed.* Otherwise, you'll see a list of the fonts already installed.

6. Click the **Add fonts...** button. You'll see the **Add fonts** dialog box, with a message reading: *Insert the disk with the font files you wish to add in drive A, or choose an alternative drive/directory.* A text box provides space for you to type a new drive and/or directory, if you don't want to use the default drive, which is drive A.

7. Enter a new drive and/or directory name, or type nothing if you want to use drive A, and then click **OK.** The right-hand list box will display the file names of the fonts available from that source (see Figure 2.4).

8. Click a font name to highlight and select it. Select as many as you like. If you change your mind about adding a specific font, click its name again to deselect it.

9. Click the **Add...** button to add the fonts. You will be prompted for the directory and path where you want the

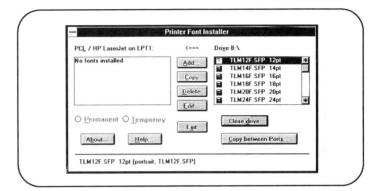

Figure 2.4: The Printer Font Installer dialog box

fonts installed for use by Windows. You can type any new directory and path you like; if the directory doesn't exist, it will be created for you.

10. Click **OK** to copy the fonts and complete the installation.

11. Click the **Close drive** button when you've completed installing the fonts.

12. If you want the fonts installed as permanent rather than temporary (the default), highlight the font names in the left-hand list box of the **Printer Font Installer** dialog box and click the **Permanent** button underneath. Temporary fonts are downloaded for printing when Windows finds them in your publications. This downloading process will cause a slight delay in printing, but allows you to use a great variety of fonts without running out of printer memory. However, if you use only a few fonts all day long, selecting **Permanent** will save you time. A line will be inserted into your AUTOEXEC.BAT file to download the fonts when you turn your computer on; they will remain in the printer memory as you proceed from job to job, with no additional delays for downloading. (The **Permanent** and **Temporary** buttons appear only if fonts are installed.)

13. When you're finished, click **Exit** to close the **Printer Font Installer** dialog box, and then click **OK** to close the other

dialog boxes you opened after clicking the **Printers** icon. Finally, close the **Control Panel** window.

If Windows is not familiar with a typeface family from which you're selecting fonts, an **Edit** dialog box will be displayed (see Figure 2.5). Here you will be asked to provide a typeface name for the font and select a family to which it belongs. The typeface name you furnish will appear on the font menus of Windows applications. The family names indicate the general appearance of the typeface and will assist Windows in generating appropriate font metrics files to measure spacing on the screen. The family names are also used in determining which existing screen font to use to represent the typeface on the screen.

Here are the family names Windows uses and how the program defines them:

- **Roman.** Proportional fonts (fonts with variable character widths) that have *serifs*. Serifs are the small lines that protrude— often at right angles —from the main lines of characters, as found in the Times Roman family. (The Windows version of Times Roman is called Tms Rmn.)

- **Swiss.** Proportional sans serif fonts (without serifs), such as the Helvetica family. (The Windows version of Helvetica is called Helv.)

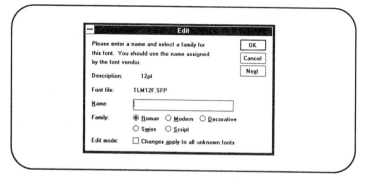

Figure 2.5: The Edit dialog box

- **Modern.** Nonproportional typefaces that resemble the output of a typewriter. (An example is Courier.)

- **Script.** Cursive fonts (look like handwriting).

- **Decorative.** Display typefaces with an ornate or unusual appearance (examples: Old English, Paintbrush, and Broadway).

Select the **Edit mode** box to provide the same typeface name and family assignment for all of your new fonts. Then click **OK.** If the new fonts require different typeface and family names, click **Next** when you've finished describing one new font, and then proceed to the next. Click **OK** when you've finished giving typeface and family names to all of them.

Installing Adobe Type Manager

Adobe Type Manager is provided in a separate package included with PageMaker 4.0. It includes outlines that will create both printer and screen fonts on demand, in any size, in these typeface families: Courier, Times, Helvetica, and Symbol. ATM will also make bold, italic, and bold italic variations of Courier, Times, and Helvetica. No bitmapped fonts are installed on your computer to accomplish this. However, you can continue to use any existing screen and printer fonts you may have.

You can also buy and install many typeface outlines that will work with ATM. The only stipulation is that they must be in the Adobe PostScript Type 1 format. Typeface outlines in this format are manufactured and sold by Adobe and several other vendors.

You don't need a PostScript printer

Here's an important point: although these outlines are in the PostScript language, you do not need a PostScript printer to use them. You can use a printer in the Hewlett-Packard LaserJet family, a dot-matrix printer, or almost any other printer supported by Windows.

Here's how to install ATM:

1. Insert the ATM disk in a floppy drive.

2. Start Windows (if it's not already active) and open the **Windows Program Manager.**

3. Pull down the **File** menu and choose the **Run...** command.

4. Type **A:INSTALL** in the **Command Line** box. (Start the command with some letter other than A if your floppy drive has a different designation.) Click **OK.** You'll see the **ATM Installer** screen (see Figure 2.6), where you will be asked to specify directories for the typeface outlines and the accompanying font metrics (.PFM) files. In most cases, you can accept the defaults of **C:\PSFONTS** and **C:\PSFONTS\PFM.**

5. Click the **Install** box to continue with the installation. If you're using a Hewlett-Packard LaserJet printer, or another printer using HP's PCL printer language, you'll be asked if you want to have PCL bitmapped fonts installed. They'll take up disk space, but they may speed up printing slightly on your system. You probably won't need them, so click the **Cancel** button. If you choose to have them installed,

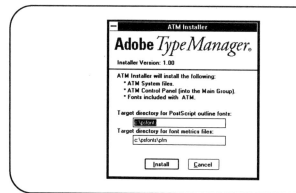

Figure 2.6: The ATM Installer screen

you'll be asked to accept the default **C:\PCLFONTS** directory to store them—or type the name of another directory. Then click **Install** to continue.

6. When the installation is complete, you will see a message confirming that fact and telling you that you must restart Windows to activate ATM. Click **OK** to leave the **Installer.**

You can easily add more Type 1 typeface outlines to Windows (and PageMaker). Here's how:

1. Click the **ATM** icon (or select the **ATMCNTRL.EXE** file). The **ATM Control Panel** will appear (see Figure 2.7).

2. Click the **Add…** button. The **Add ATM Fonts** dialog box will appear.

3. Select the drive containing the additional outlines.

4. Select the outlines you want installed by clicking on them from the list of displayed typefaces (see Figure 2.8), and then click the **Add** button. When the installation is complete, you'll be returned to the **ATM Control Panel.**

5. Click **Exit** to complete the installation, and then restart Windows so the additions will take effect.

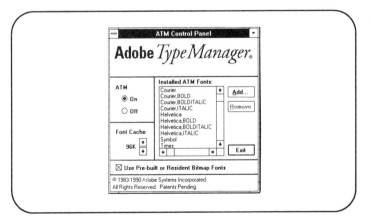

Figure 2.7: The ATM Control Panel

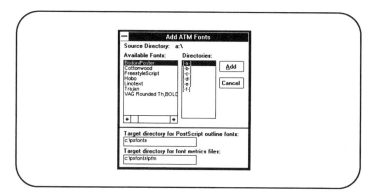

Figure 2.8: The Add ATM Fonts dialog box

There are four other options on the **ATM Control Panel** that affect the installation and operation of typefaces:

- **ATM.** This option has **On** and **Off** buttons for activating and deactivating ATM. (If you wanted to run a program that was incompatible with ATM, you might want to disable ATM temporarily.)

- **Font cache.** The default font cache is 96K. You can use the arrows to decrease the cache to as little as 64K or increase it to as much as 8192K, depending upon whether you're short of memory or have plenty of RAM. If you're using many typefaces, a larger cache may improve performance.

- **Use Pre-built or Resident Bitmap Fonts.** The default is to have this box selected so that ATM will recognize bitmapped typefaces on your system. Click the box to deselect it if you want Windows and PageMaker to use only ATM typefaces.

- **Remove.** Select this option to remove ATM typefaces from your system. Outlines removed will no longer be displayed on font menus, but the files will still be stored on your hard disk unless you erase them.

To make newly installed fonts and outlines show up on the font menus of your Windows applications and accessories, you will probably have to display the printer setup dialog box for each application, select the fonts option (if available—even though you'll really make no changes), and then click **OK** or its equivalent as needed to back out of the menus and save the revisited printer setup. This procedure will cause the application to recheck the WIN.INI file, where Windows font information is stored. After the application has been updated in this fashion, the new fonts will appear on its menu.

Other Font Installation Options

Bitstream's FaceLift for Windows operates much the same as ATM, creating matching screen and printer fonts on the fly from outlines. A large library of typefaces is available.

For some years Bitstream has provided another font system called Fontware; it can make bitmapped screen and printer fonts in any size you specify and has a special installation kit for Windows. You must have Fontware version 3.0 or later to install fonts into Windows 3.0. Fontware does not create fonts on the fly—with the exception that it can make PostScript-compatible printer outlines for use on PostScript printers. If you already have a library of Fontware typefaces, you can obtain FaceLift versions for a modest upgrade price. However, existing Fontware typefaces do not work with FaceLift.

AGFA Compugraphic and Hewlett-Packard both market Type Director, which (like Fontware) can make and install bitmapped screen and printer fonts into Windows 3.0. Type Director does not create PostScript outlines; however, it will make scalable typefaces for an HP LaserJet III printer.

Step 3
Starting a Publication

If you'd like to combine type with graphics and create a quick flyer or announcement with PageMaker, you don't have to make elaborate preparations or even specify margin and column sizes. To produce a one-page document on regular letter-sized paper, you can use most of the program's standard settings and just charge ahead. PageMaker is *object oriented*—meaning that each text or graphic element you add is considered a separate object; you can simply create or import text or graphics, resize these objects and drag them around on the page until the layout pleases you, and then issue your print command. Presto! You have a publication.

You can create simple publications right away

However, you do need to know a few basics first—such as what can be found in each of the menus and the meaning and function of the various parts of the display. You'll cover these fundamentals in this Step; then Step 4 will explain the text and drawing tools and Step 5 will deal with importing and sizing graphics. At that point you will be able to create one-column, one-page documents for many purposes.

In the following Steps, you will learn how to produce more elaborate publications.

Opening PageMaker and Using Page Setup

You must open Windows 3.0 first in order to load PageMaker. Since the Windows installation program will have added your Windows directory to the path command of your AUTOEXEC.BAT file, you can open Windows from the DOS prompt of any of your drives or directories.

The procedure for starting Windows and loading PageMaker is as follows:

1. Type **WIN**, and then press **Enter** from the DOS prompt of any drive or directory. The **Windows Program Manager**

window will appear. (If you don't see this window, you will
see its icon at the bottom of your screen; double-click the
icon to open the window.) A row of *group icons* will be
displayed at the bottom of the Program Manager window;
the PageMaker installation program will have added an
Aldus group icon to this row, as shown in Figure 3.1.
Group icons provide a convenient way of starting related
applications from within Windows.

2.   Double-click the **Aldus** group icon. The **Aldus** group window will open. Within this window are icons to run both
the Aldus Setup program and PageMaker itself.

3.   Double-click the **PageMaker** icon. PageMaker will start.
You will see the Aldus logo and copyright notice, and then
a menu bar at the top of an otherwise blank window.

4.   Pull down the **File** menu, and select the first option, **New...**
(a shortcut is **Ctrl-N**). Now you will see the **Page setup**
dialog box shown in Figure 3.2 (although your target
printer may be different).

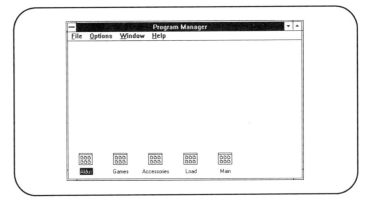

*Figure 3.1: The Windows Program Manager window, showing the
Aldus group icon*

Page setup is where you establish some of the size specifications
for your publication. In PageMaker you do this for a new publication before you create it.

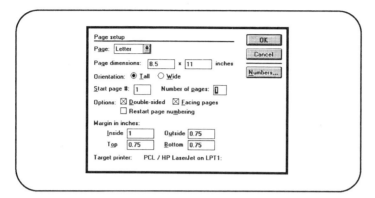

Figure 3.2: The Page setup dialog box

Here is an explanation of the options in this dialog box:

- **Page** is where you specify the page size you want. Here the default size is **Letter**, the normal, letter-size, 8½ by 11-inch page. You can select other options by placing the mouse pointer on the down arrow to the right of the word **Letter** and pressing to display a small drop-down menu with these additional choices: **Legal**, which prints on 8½ by 14-inch legal-size paper; **Tabloid** (11 by 17 inches), which you would use if you wanted to prepare files to be used by a service bureau or printshop to print a tabloid-size newspaper; and **Custom**, which permits you to type other measurements in the two **Page dimensions** boxes. For example, you might want to specify a smaller page size for the printing of an instruction manual, or a larger size for a poster. The maximum size supported is 17 by 22 inches. If you need to work with a European or Japanese page size (they're slightly different from U.S. standard sizes), you can enter those dimensions too.

- **Orientation** offers two button choices and refers to the way you want the document printed on the page. The default is **Tall** (called *portrait* mode in many PC applications), where the document is printed across the short dimension of the page, as you would normally type a letter. The alternative is **Wide** (often called *landscape* mode),

which causes the document to be printed across the long
dimension of the page, so you need to turn the paper side-
ways to read it.

- **Start page #** lets you establish your page numbering. The
default is to number the first page 1; however, if the file to
be created is actually the continuation of a book manuscript, you can start at the number after the page number
you ended with previously.

- **Number of pages** is simply the number of pages in the
publication. Once you have established a figure here
(the default is 1), you can change it only by using the
Insert pages... or **Remove pages...** commands from the
Page menu.

- **Options** is where you click to select a box if your publication is to be double-sided. If you have clicked the **Double-
sided** box, an **X** appears in it. Then you click the second
box in this section, **Facing pages**, if you want to work
with facing pages (left and right), instead of seeing only
one page at a time. Click **Restart page numbering** to
restart page numbering within a publication.

- **Margin in inches** has four boxes, where you can type values for **Inside, Outside, Top,** and **Bottom** margins, if you
don't want to accept the defaults.

You click the **Numbers...** box on the screen to change the default
page-numbering system (which is simply 1, 2, 3, and so on).
You'll learn how to do this in Step 8.

At the bottom of this dialog box, the name of the currently selected printer is displayed.

Click **OK** when you've completed your changes in the dialog box.
If you want to create a simple one-page announcement, you may
need no changes, except to be sure that the **Double-sided** and
Facing pages boxes are not selected. (If you click the **Double-
sided** box when an X appears in it, the X disappears from that box
and from the **Facing pages** box as well, deselecting both boxes.)

Touring the PageMaker Screen

As soon as you click **OK** to save your changes to the **Page setup** dialog box, the PageMaker *pasteboard* appears (see Figure 3.3); this is the main area of the display, where you work on your publications. Centered on the pasteboard is a page that is initially empty, except for a rectangle representing its margins. If you've selected the **Double-sided** and **Facing pages** boxes, you see *two* empty pages, side by side.

You won't always see two pages, even if you've selected **Facing pages**. Page 1 is always considered a single right-hand page, so it will appear by itself. If you have a total of only 2 pages in your publication, page 2 will also appear by itself—since it is considered to be a left-hand page, which would be followed only by a facing right-hand page 3. In fact, any final left-hand page will appear by itself. In other circumstances, you will always see left and right facing pages when the option is selected.

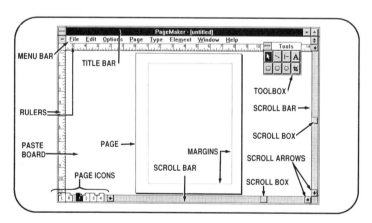

Figure 3.3: The PageMaker screen

Above the pasteboard you'll see the *menu bar,* surmounted by a *title bar* for the window, which (in accordance with the standard Windows interface) displays the name of the application (**Page-Maker**), followed by the word **Untitled** until the document is first saved and named. The pasteboard itself is framed by *rulers* on its top and left sides, and by *scroll bars* on its right and bottom sides.

Rulers let you measure the placement of the items on your page. The rulers are calibrated in inches—unless you change the measurement standard with the **Preferences** command on the **Edit** menu. Other ruler options include measuring in inches decimal, millimeters, picas (and points), or ciceros (a European standard).

How to use scroll bars

Scroll bars are a standard Windows feature that let you move the display so you can see different portions of a page that is too large to fit onto the screen in its entirety. The scroll bars work the same in PageMaker as in other Windows applications:

- To scroll one line, click a scroll arrow.

- To scroll the display one windowful in any direction, click a scroll bar on the appropriate side of its scroll box.

- To scroll part way through a document, drag the scroll box up or down with the mouse. For example, to move a third of the way into the document, drag the scroll box to a position a third of the way along the scroll bar.

- To scroll continuously, place the scroll pointer on a scroll arrow and hold down the left button.

The PageMaker Menus

The PageMaker pull-down menus are named **File, Edit, Options, Page, Type, Element, Window**, and **Help**. In this section, you'll receive a brief introduction to each.

- The **File** menu contains typical Windows options, including commands to open, close, save, and print documents. You can also change your selection of an active printer. Additional commands are specific to PageMaker. **Place...** is used to import text or graphics files and place them in your publication. **Links...** lets you link external documents so they can be printed as a part of a publication, including the latest modifications to those files. **Revert** eliminates all changes since you last saved your publication—handy if you realize you've just ruined some important element that still exists in the previous version. **Export...** is for exporting text from PageMaker publications to other programs; it translates PageMaker text into your choice of several other formats, including ASCII, Microsoft Word, and Windows Write. **Book...** calls up a dialog box where you can list all of the publication file names that are part of a book; performing this action lets PageMaker prepare a table of contents and index that will include all parts of the book and print the entire book in sequence.

- The **Edit** menu contains Windows editing commands to undo your latest action; to cut, copy, paste, and clear selected objects; and to select all objects in the document. Also, the **Edit** menu is where you access the **Preferences** dialog box, where you can specify how PageMaker will display certain features of the program while you work; these include the measurement system to be used for the rulers and whether graphics are to be shown in *high resolution* (making you wait frequently while the screen is redrawn), *normal,* or *gray out* (the fastest mode because you see a gray rectangle instead of the actual graphic). In addition, it's through the **Edit** menu that you access the Story editor (the program's mini word processor, explained in Step 11), find and replace text, and check spelling.

- The **Options** menu is where you elect whether or not to show rulers and guide lines that help you position text and graphic objects, and is also where you stipulate whether or not you want objects to align themselves automatically to these gauges. From this menu you can also lock guides so they can't be moved accidentally, make text flow automatically from column to column, and create indexes and tables of contents. (Note that the Story editor also has an **Options** menu, with different choices.)

- The **Page** menu lets you zoom in and out on the current page, go to a specific page, insert and delete pages, and control some functions relating to *master pages* (explained in Step 7). (The **Page** menu is not available when you're using the Story editor.)

- The **Type** menu is where you select typefaces and control how they're handled (see Step 4). Here you also control features relating to paragraphs, indentations, tabstops, hyphenation, and justification (centering text, displaying it flush left, and so on).

- The **Element** menu covers several options: line widths and patterns to be used with PageMaker's drawing tools, text rotation and word-wrapping from line to line, displaying objects in the foreground or behind other objects, adjusting the appearance of graphic images including the corners of rectangles, colors to be applied to objects for printing, and some file-linking features.

- The **Window** menu has commands to display or hide the toolbox, scroll bars, and style and color palettes. You can also use this menu to execute some standard Windows commands: switch from one window to another, rearrange the display of icons automatically when window sizes change, and cause multiple windows to be displayed either as slightly overlapping so part of each is visible (the **Cascade** command) or so that equal portions of each are displayed (the **Tile** command).

- The **Help** menu contains indexed information about Page-Maker commands and features.

Page Icons

At the lower left corner of the PageMaker display, you'll find icons representing both master pages and the regular pages of a publication (unless you've turned off the display of the scroll bars through the **Window** menu). (See Figure 3.4.)

If you haven't selected **Facing pages** in the Page setup dialog box, you'll see only one master-page icon, labeled **R**; if you *are* working with facing pages, there will be two master-page icons, labeled **L** and **R** (for Left and Right). To the right of these icons will be additional icons numbered for each page in your publication; if there are too many pages for the icons to be shown on the screen, small arrows will appear which you can scroll to display additional page icons. You click an icon to display that particular page so you can work on it. (If you have a very large document, the **Go to page**... command on the **Page** menu is usually a faster way to select a page far removed from the current one.)

These are the main elements of the PageMaker screen, with the exception of the toolbox, which is explained in Step 4. You'll learn more about the menus and commands in later Steps, as they're used to help accomplish specific tasks.

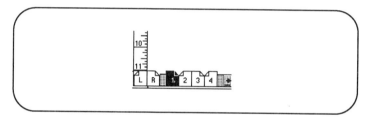

Figure 3.4: The page icons

Step 4
Using Text & Drawing Tools

The PageMaker toolbox (**Tools** menu) appears in the form of a small window that is positioned by default in the upper right area of the pasteboard (see Figure 4.1). You can drag it by its title bar to any other location on your screen, or click its close box to hide it when it's not needed. With its tools, you can add text to your publication and draw lines, ovals, circles, rectangles, and squares. You can also add a fill pattern to the graphic objects you create (with a separate **Fill** command).

The tool shaped like an arrow is the **pointer;** it's used to select text blocks and graphic objects and to deselect other tools.

Selecting Typefaces and Using the Text Tool

You can add text anywhere on your current page by clicking the **text** tool (it is a capital letter A), and then clicking where you want to start typing. However, you'll want to select your typeface and size first.

Picking Typefaces and How They'll Appear

You have access to whatever typefaces have been installed in Windows (see Step 2). To select a typeface, follow these steps:

1. Pull down the **Type** menu, and select **Font.** You'll see the list of typefaces currently installed in your copy of Windows for the active printer (see Figure 4.2). Choose the typeface you want.

2. Pull down the **Type** menu again, and select **Size.** You'll see a list of installed sizes from which you can choose. If you're using a PostScript printer or a typeface utility that lets you generate font sizes on the fly from outlines, you can select the **Other…** command. A small window will appear where you can type a size not shown on the menu, from 4 pt. to 650 pt.

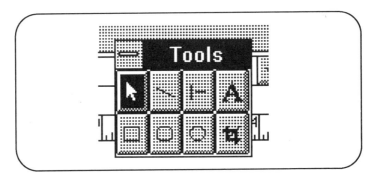

Figure 4.1: The Toolbox

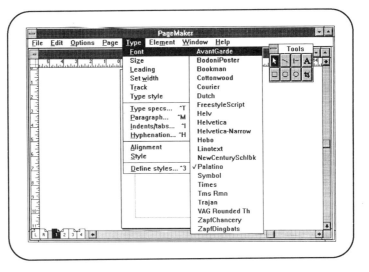

Figure 4.2: The Font submenu for a PostScript printer

3.   If you want to add an attribute such as boldface or italics to the font you'll use, you can pull down the **Type** menu a third time, select **Type style**, and then pick the attribute you want. You can select this menu option more than once to combine attributes. For example, you can make a typeface bold italic by choosing **Bold,** and then returning to the

menu and choosing **Italic**. Selected options are preceded by a checkmark.

If you want to select a typeface, change the current point size, and change its style all at the same time (not an unusual circumstance), the fastest way to do this is to use another submenu, instead of following steps 1, 2, and 3 above. Pull down the **Type** menu and select the **Type specs...** command. You'll be able to make all of these choices (and more) at one time, from the **Type specifications** dialog box (see Figure 4.3). A shortcut for calling up this dialog box from your publication is simply to press **Ctrl-T**.

There are additional items on the **Type** menu that let you adjust *kerning* (the spacing between specific pairs of characters), *leading* (the spacing between lines), *alignment* (how the text in a paragraph is justified—left, right, etc.), *hyphenation* (when and how words are divided with hyphens), and other features. For simple documents, you can probably use the default settings on these options.

When you add text, you'll want to be sure that the words you type are legible and not "greeked"—shown as simulated text or gray areas instead of the actual words. PageMaker by default "greeks" small-sized text in some page-display sizes. If you can't read the text you type, simply pull down the **Page** menu and select an

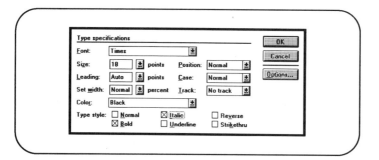

Figure 4.3: The Type specifications dialog box

option such as **Actual size** to enlarge the display of the portion of the page on which you're working.

Entering and Positioning Text

Once you've selected a typeface in the style and size you want, use this procedure to enter and position your text:

1. Click the **text** tool (the **A**) to activate it. It will become highlighted, and the cursor will assume the shape of an I-beam.

2. Move the cursor to the area where you want the text to appear, and click. If you haven't specified multiple columns on a master page (see Step 7), a flashing vertical line will appear at the left margin of the page, at the vertical position where you've clicked. (As an alternative to starting text entry by clicking, you can drag to form a rectangle for the text block, as explained in the next paragraph.)

3. Type the text. By default, the text will wrap automatically to the next line when it reaches the right margin. If you're using a small font size and haven't established multiple columns, this default process will probably result in a line length too long for easy reading. You can press **Enter** when necessary to keep the lines short. However, there's an easier way to control your line length: you can place the cursor at the location where you want the text to start; instead of clicking, press the left mouse button and drag to the right. A rectangle will appear; release the mouse button when the rectangle is the approximate size you want for the text block. When you establish a rectangle for a text block in this manner, text entry will start at the position where you began dragging, not at the left margin of the page. As you type, the text will now wrap from line to line, using the right side of the rectangle as the right margin.

4. When you've finished typing the text, click the **pointer** tool to deselect the **text** tool. You've now finished creating a text object.

5. To move or reshape the text object, click the **pointer** any-
    where on the words you typed. The block of text will be
    selected— enclosed by four small square blocks called
    handles, which mark its boundaries; you can drag any one
    of these handles to reshape the block of text. Above and
    below the block will be a horizontal line with a tab-shaped
    handle centered on it; these line-tab combinations are
    called *windowshades* (see Figure 4.4). You can "roll" either
    windowshade up or down to display more or less of the text
    block; if all of the text is not displayed, an arrow will ap-
    pear in the bottom windowshade handle to indicate that
    more text is available. You move the text block by position-
    ing the pointer within the block and dragging the object to
    its new location. See Step 9 for a more complete explana-
    tion of placing text.

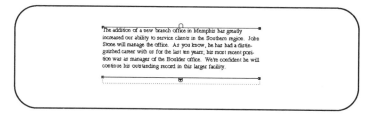

Figure 4.4: A text block with windowshades

Using the Drawing Tools

The remainder of the icons in the toolbox represent drawing tools,
with the exception of the **cropping** tool, located at the lower right
corner of the toolbox; this tool is used to select a portion of an imported graphic, "cropping" the image for display and publication.
Its use will be described in Step 5.

The drawing tools are not intended for the creation of freehand ar-
tistic sketches or architectural floor plans. They let you create
rules between columns and draw lines and boxes to emphasize
and enhance text, as well as graphics created in other programs.
You can adjust the line width of your drawings and add fill patterns to closed objects such as rectangles and circles.

Changing Drawing Defaults

By default, PageMaker draws a solid line one point in width, with all of the drawing tools. You can pull down the **Element** menu and select **Line** to change the default to your choice of several dashed or double lines in widths ranging from a hairline to 12 points (see Figure 4.5).

By default, there is no fill in any closed figure you draw, such as a rectangle or circle. This means that the interior of the figure will be transparent. Pull down the **Element** menu and select **Fill** to see the available choices for fill patterns. The first choice (below **None**) is **Paper,** which creates a solid white fill that is *not* transparent. The second choice is **Solid,** which can be modified by choosing a percentage of black (a shade of gray) for the fill.

Below these solid-fill choices, you'll find a variety of patterns you can select.

Bring to front and Send to back commands

In PageMaker, fills are often used as a background for text. However, when you create a closed figure to highlight text in this way, it will appear on top of the text, hiding it, if you draw it after the text block has been completed. Even if you draw the figure in

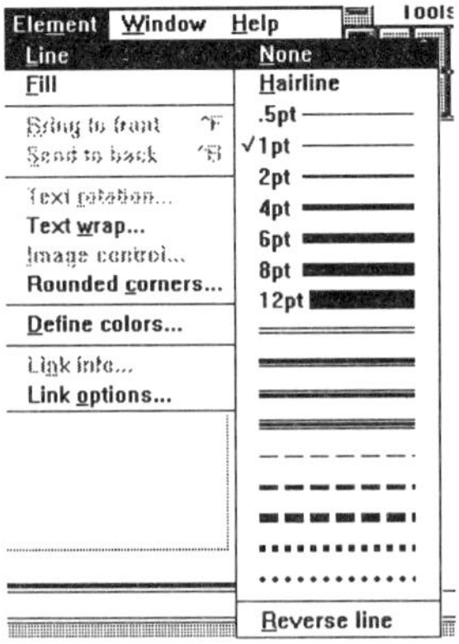

Figure 4.5: Choices on the Line submenu

another part of the pasteboard and then drag it to its final location, it will still be shown on top of the text.

This problem can easily be corrected. Here's how:

1. Click the figure to select it.

2. Pull down the **Element** menu and select the **Send to back** command. The figure will now move to the background, displayed behind the text block (see Figure 4.6). The reverse command, **Bring to front**, will bring a selected object in the foreground, with other objects displayed behind it. (Shortcuts are pressing **Ctrl-B** from your publication for **Send to back** and **Ctrl-F** for **Bring to front**.)

If you want to readjust a filled figure's position after you've issued the **Send to back** command (which places it in the background behind a text block), note that selecting the figure again and moving it will bring it to the front, hiding the text. The fastest way to correctly align the background behind text is to draw the background figure with no fill pattern; with the area inside the figure's boundaries transparent, you can see the text and position the

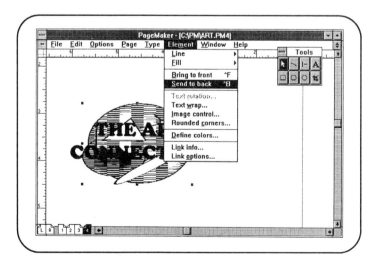

Figure 4.6: Placing a background behind text

figure around the text exactly where you want it. When the two objects are correctly placed in relation to each other, add the pattern to the figure and then issue the **Send to back** command.

Another option on the **Element** menu is the **Rounded corners...** command; its dialog box displays six kinds of rounded corners you can choose to apply to squares and rectangles.

Any change you make to the **Line, Fill,** and **Rounded corners...** defaults will be applied to all of your subsequent drawings in the current publication—until you select the menu option and make a different selection. You can reselect a completed object and change the attributes you've applied to it, and you can resize the object by dragging one of its handles.

Using the Diagonal Line Tool

The **diagonal line** tool is represented in the toolbox by the diagonal line next to the **pointer** arrow. With this tool, you can draw a straight line at any angle. The line will be straight, even if you don't drag the mouse in a straight line. If you hold down the **Shift** key while you draw with this tool, it will draw only lines that are strictly horizontal, vertical, or at a 45-degree angle to the perpendicular, making it perform exactly as the **perpendicular line** tool, described next.

Using the Perpendicular Line Tool

The **perpendicular line** tool draws only vertical or horizontal lines, or lines at a 45-degree angle. Holding down the **Shift** key has no effect on the operation of this tool.

Using the Square Corner Tool

The **square corner** tool draws rectangles with square corners. If you hold down the **Shift** key as you drag the mouse, the tool will make perfect squares.

Using the Rounded Corner Tool

The **rounded corner** tool draws rectangles with rounded corners. Like the **square corner** tool, it will draw squares if you hold down the **Shift** key as you drag.

Figure 4.7 shows a rectangle made with the **rounded corner** tool and a line width of 6 pt. Its use is typical; it forms a frame for an imported illustration.

Using the Oval Tool

The **oval** tool draws ovals. If you hold down the **Shift** key as you drag, it will make circles.

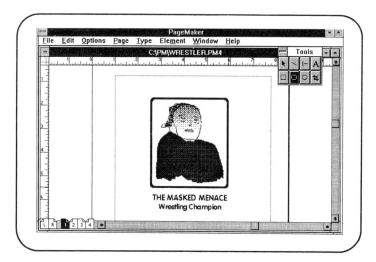

Figure 4.7: An illustration framed by using the rounded corner tool

Step 5
Importing & Sizing Graphics

15

You can add illustrations to your PageMaker documents in several ways. First of all, you can use Paintbrush (the basic paint program included with every copy of Microsoft Windows) to draw simple graphics yourself and bring them into PageMaker through the Windows clipboard (which is explained later in this Step). You can also use the clipboard to insert graphics from third-party programs that are also Windows applications; these include the highly rated CorelDRAW, Micrografx Designer and Charisma, and Arts & Letters Graphics Editor.

PageMaker can read and import most popular graphics formats—paint and drawing files, spreadsheet graphs, and images produced by scanners. However, the files must have the expected extension in order to be recognized by the program. For example, a file in the TIFF format (produced by most scanners) requires a .TIF extension.

Placing a Graphic in Your Publication

You import a graphic image by using the **Place…** command on the **File** menu, also used for importing text files. This is the sequence:

1. Pull down the **File** menu and select **Place…** (A shortcut is to press **Ctrl-D**.) You'll see the **Place file** box. The first item in its list box will be highlighted (unless there are no placeable files in the current directory). If the item is a text file, the first option in the **Place:** area of the dialog box will read **As new item,** and the button for that option will already be selected. However, if the first item in the list box is a graphic file, or if you use the mouse to move the highlighting to a graphic file, the **Place:** selections will be different. The first will read **As independent graphic** —usually the choice you'll want. The other graphic choices appear in the dialog box only when applicable. **Replacing entire graphic** replaces a selected existing graphic with

your new selection and **As inline graphic** inserts the new graphic as part of an existing text flow if you've clicked an insertion point in the story.

2.   Highlight the graphic file you want to insert, changing to another directory or drive to select it, if necessary (see Figure 5.1).

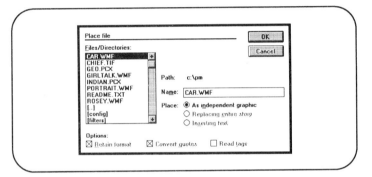

Figure 5.1: The Place file dialog box

3.   If necessary, change the default **As independent graphic** to **Replacing entire graphic** or **As inline graphic,** by clicking the appropriate button. Then click **OK**. The dialog box will disappear, and the pointer (cursor) will change into an icon representing the upper left corner of the graphic image. The appearance of the icon will reflect the type of format it represents: paint (symbolized by a paint-brush), draw (shown as a pencil), scanned image (depicted by a square filled with dots), TIF graphic (represented by an X in a square), or Encapsulated PostScript file (indi-cated by the letters **PS**).

4.   Move the cursor to the spot on the current page where you want to place the upper left corner of the graphic image, and click. The image will appear at that location.

Sizing a Graphic Image

If the graphic image you've imported doesn't fit the space you've planned for it, you can easily resize it—either keeping the same proportions by changing both height and width simultaneously or distorting the image by changing only one dimension.

Follow this procedure to distort the image:

1. Click the graphic to select it. It will become enclosed by eight small square black handles—one at each corner of the image and one centered on each of the four sides (see Figure 5.2).

2. Place the pointer on one of the corner handles and hold down the left mouse button.

3. When the pointer becomes a double-headed arrow, drag in the direction you want to expand or contract the image. If you drag to the left or right, the height of the image remains unchanged. If you drag up or down, the width of the image remains unchanged. If you drag diagonally, both dimensions are distorted.

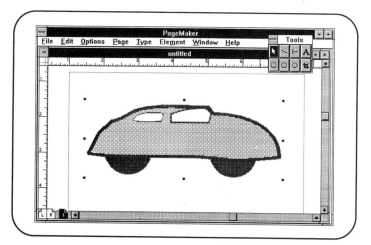

Figure 5.2: A selected graphic, showing its eight handles

4. To be sure you change only the height or the width, drag a center handle.

5. Release the mouse button when the appearance of the image is what you want.

To resize the image without distorting it, simply hold down the **Shift** key as you drag a corner handle. Both dimensions will be enlarged or reduced simultaneously. Figure 5.3 illustrates the difference between resizing to distort or to retain the original proportions.

If you don't like the result of a resizing operation, you can restore the graphic to its previous appearance in two ways:

1. If you want to cancel the resizing immediately after completing it, pull down the **Edit** menu and select the first option, **Undo**. Provided you haven't performed some other action after the resizing, the **Undo** command will return the image to its previous shape. (**Undo** will only cancel out the most recent action.) There's a shortcut for the **Undo** command: just press **Alt-Backspace**.

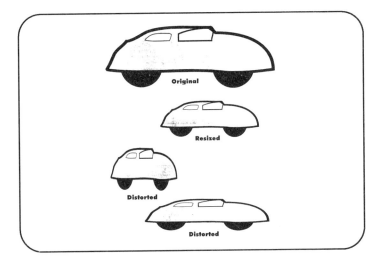

Figure 5.3: Comparison of resized and distorted graphics

2. If you decide you want to restore the original appearance of a distorted image, click the graphic to select it, and then hold down the **Shift** key as you drag a corner handle. The original proportions will be reestablished. However, the original size of the image will be restored only if you drag the image until it is exactly that size.

Cropping a Graphic Image

If you want to display only a portion of an imported graphic, use the cropping tool, which is in the lower right corner of the toolbox. Here's how:

1. Click the icon for the **cropping** tool. It will become highlighted, and the pointer will assume the same shape as the icon.

2. Click the graphic to select it, and place the **cropping** tool over one of the corner handles of the image so the corner shows through the center of the tool.

3. Drag the image to reduce it to the size you want. You will make part of the image disappear as you create the smaller size, rather than shrinking the graphic. Release the mouse button.

4. Now place the pointer in the middle of the remaining portion of the graphic and hold down the left mouse button again. Drag to observe the result. You'll discover that the portion of the graphic still visible on your page is actually being shown in a window. You can drag the entire image until the part you want is displayed. That's how you crop a graphic in PageMaker.

5. Release the mouse button when the image is cropped to your satisfaction.

Step 6
Changing the Page Display

Now that you know how to use the text and drawing tools and how to import graphics, you can produce simple one-page, one-column documents in PageMaker very easily.

Figure 6.1 is an example; it shows a flyer being created for a mythical pizza service, consisting at this point of only two objects: a heading, and an illustration that was created in CorelDRAW and imported. The flyer is displayed in PageMaker's **Fit in window** mode, which centers the entire active page (or pages, if you're using facing pages) on the screen, with some of the pasteboard also visible. This is the default display.

There are several other display choices for your publications; they involve zooming out or zooming in to show more or less of your working area. These display choices help you "step back" to view the changes you've made to the overall layout or to see everything on the pasteboard at the same time. You can also move in closer so you can fine-tune text and make graphic adjustments.

Figure 6.1: A flyer displayed with the Fit in window command

These are the display options, all accessed from the **Page** menu:

- Pick **Fit in world** to show all of the active page (or pages) displayed on the entire pasteboard (see Figure 6.2). This choice is handy if you want to see objects stored on the pasteboard that you haven't dragged into place on a page yet. This command is accessed by holding down the **Shift** key while selecting **Fit in window**; **Fit in World** will then replace the **Fit in window** command. (However, you will not see **Fit in World** in your menu.)

- Pick **Fit in window** to center the entire active page(s) on the screen and show a portion of the surrounding pasteboard.

- Pick **25% size** to show the active page(s) at 25% of actual size. If the page size you're using is 8½ by 11 inches, this choice displays only slightly less of the pasteboard than the **Fit in world** command does.

- Pick **50% size** or **75% size** to show the active page(s) at 50% or 75% of actual size. One of these settings is usually a good choice when you want to draw rules between columns.

- Pick **Actual size** to show the active page(s) at the size at which the publication will be printed. Since the printed page is usually larger than the computer screen, this choice will probably require scrolling to see all of the page, but it gives you the opportunity to evaluate how elements will appear in their final printed form.

- Pick **200% size** or **400% size** to show the active page(s) at 200% or 400% of actual size. These choices will enlarge the display so you can place objects more precisely.

Figure 6.2 shows the pizza flyer displayed with the **Fit in world** command. In this mode, because the entire pasteboard is visible, you can see that there is a third object available to be added to the page—a slogan.

Figure 6.3 shows the same page at 50% size, with the slogan dragged into its final position.

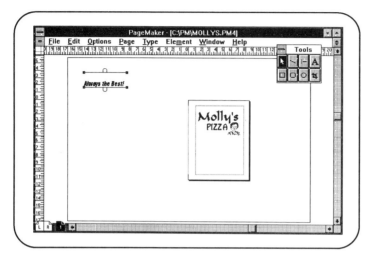

Figure 6.2: The same flyer displayed with the Fit in world command, revealing a slogan on the pasteboard

Figure 6.3: The same flyer at 50% actual size, with the slogan added

Step 7

Creating Master Pages

To create a document of more than one page, you'll want to create *master pages*. These pages are never printed by themselves. They contain elements that you want repeated on the regular pages of your publication. Examples would be headers with automatic page numbering, a company logo, or the *layout grid*—the nonprinting network of guide lines that lets you place columns of text and graphics precisely and uniformly on your pages.

Your publication might not use facing pages. Perhaps it's a company report that will be printed on only one side of each sheet of paper. In this case, you need only *one* master page.

However, most multipage publications are printed on both sides of the paper. In that case, you'll want to work with *two* master pages—one for left-hand (even-numbered) pages and the other for right-hand (odd-numbered) pages.

Why two master pages? One reason is the fact that you'll probably want a wide *right* margin on the left-hand page and a wide *left* margin on the right-hand page; the combination will create an adequate *gutter,* a wider margin between facing pages to allow for the folding and binding of the pages.

Another reason for two master pages is that you'll probably want the appearance of facing pages to vary. For instance, the name of the publication or a section might appear on the left-hand pages, with the name of the current chapter on the right-hand pages. In addition, page numbers are usually shown near the outer margin of both left-hand and right-hand pages so that the reader can easily locate a particular page.

Once you establish master-page elements, you don't have to apply them to every odd or even page of your publication. You can modify or change elements on any individual page.

Establishing Preferences

Before you set up master pages, you should make any changes you want in the **Preferences** dialog box. As mentioned in Step 3, this is where you establish the measurement system you want to use for the current publication—in other words, whether you want to measure areas on your pages in inches or by some other standard. There are several other options in this dialog box (shown in Figure 7.1). To access it, pull down the **Edit** menu, and select the **Preferences...** command.

Here is an explanation of the choices in the **Preferences** dialog box:

- **Measurement system** provides a drop-down list from which you can select the measurement system you want: inches (the default), inches decimal, millimeters, picas and points, or ciceros. Click the down arrow next to the current selection to see the other alternatives. Highlight one of these standards to select it; it will now be used for measurements with the horizontal ruler and in these dialog boxes: **Page setup, Paragraph attributes,** and **Spacing attributes.** You set the standard for the vertical ruler separately (discussed below). (You may find *inches decimal* an unfamiliar term; when you choose this option, inches are divided into units divisible by ten.)

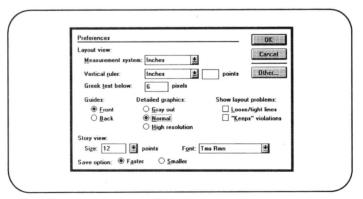

Figure 7.1: The Preferences dialog box

- **Vertical ruler** lets you use a different measurement standard for the vertical ruler. Why would you want this feature? One example: some users like to measure most objects in inches; however, they prefer to measure lines of text in picas and points. (You can change these standards as often as you like in your publication, as long as you realize that objects created before you've changed the measurement system may not properly align to the new standard.) The options provided in the **Vertical ruler** drop-down list are the same as for **Measurement system** and are selected in the same way, except that there is also a **Custom** option. When you choose **Custom**, you can enter a point size in the box to the right of the **Vertical ruler** box; the purpose of this option is to let you enter a figure that matches the *leading* (the spacing between your lines) that you're using. When the leading and the vertical ruler are set for the same number, the baseline of text entered afterwards will align with the tick marks on the ruler. (The *baseline* is an imaginary line on which the base of each capital letter rests.)

- **Greek text below** is set for a default value of six pixels (a *pixel* being one dot, the smallest individually-addressable element on your screen). This means that on-screen characters taking up less space than the default will be "greeked"; that is, the actual characters are represented by symbols in some screen views, allowing the screen to be redrawn faster. You can type in a new Greek text value, but most users find the default setting satisfactory. Type smaller than six pixels is hard to read on a computer screen anyway.

- **Guides:** is the next option; it has two settings: **Front** (the default) or **Back**. If **Front** is selected, the nonprinting margin, column, and ruler guides are displayed in front of the text and graphics on your pages and can be easily readjusted. When **Back** is selected, guides are displayed behind text and graphics, making them harder to move unintentionally.

- **Detailed graphics:** lets you display graphic elements in one of three ways. **Gray out** provides the fastest screen display of your pages—since graphics are represented by gray forms instead of the actual images, which take much longer to redraw on the screen. **Normal** is the default—a slower, low-resolution depiction of the images; you can see what they are, but they won't look their best on the screen. **High resolution** gives your images the best display, but will retard the redrawing of your screen considerably.

- **Show layout problems:** has two options you can select to have PageMaker call your attention to lines of text that violate common layout principles. If you select **Loose/tight lines**, lines containing text that either has too much or too little spacing between words or characters will be highlighted; you can then adjust the contents of the lines to correct the problems. If you select **"Keeps" violations**, lines that do not adhere to choices you've made in the **Paragraph specifications** dialog box (accessed from the **Type** menu) will be highlighted. The **Paragraph specifications** dialog box is where you can indicate the minimum number of lines of a paragraph you want displayed at the top or bottom of a page (called *widow* and *orphan* control) and other settings, such as how you want paragraphs split in adjoining columns. Again, you can change the contents of the highlighted lines to correct the problems.

- **Story view:** is where you can pick the typeface and size you want used when the **Story view** (PageMaker's mini word-processor) of your publication is selected. The default size is 12 pt.; you can type a different point size. The default typeface is Courier, displayed in a drop-down list box. Click the down arrow in this box to see the list of other available typefaces installed in your version of Windows; highlight another typeface to select it. (For convenience, you might want to select a typeface such as Times Roman, if you were using that particular typeface regularly in your documents and creating the text in **Story view** rather than importing it.)

- **Save option** has two buttons. The default selection is **Faster**, which saves your files quickly, as if you had picked the **Save** command. Click the other option, **Smaller**, if you want files saved as if you had chosen the **Save As** command.

The **Smaller** option creates a file that takes up less space on your hard disk.

- **Other...** is the final option in the dialog box. Press the button with this label and you'll call up another dialog box named **Screen font options**. It contains two options. **Stretch text above:** is the text size above which Page-Maker will stop using screen fonts without alteration and start stretching existing bitmapped fonts to simulate the correct appearance of larger size fonts on the screen for faster screen display. The other option is **Vector text above:**, the text size above which PageMaker will stop using screen fonts and start using *vector fonts* (that is, PageMaker's built-in outline font files) to simulate those larger sizes. Both options are set by default at 24 pixels. However, if you're using Adobe Type Manager, you can reset both of these items to 500 or more pixels, since (starting with version 4.0) PageMaker supports the use of fonts as large as 650 pt. (If you're also using fonts from other sources though, such as bitmapped fonts, you may want to retain the default values.)

Click **OK** to save any changes you've made in this dialog box, or click **Cancel** to return to your publication without changing the previous settings.

Now click the **L** or **R** icon to select either the left or right master page so you can create the basic structure for the layout of your regular pages. If you're working with facing pages, clicking either one of these icons will cause both master pages to be displayed side by side.

Setting the Zero Point

Once you've chosen a measurement standard, you need to consider the placement of the *zero point,* the intersection of the zeros on the horizontal and vertical rulers. This is the point from which you will measure positions on your pages. In a publication with single-sided pages, the default zero point is where the top and left edges of the page meet; if you're using facing pages, the default zero point is where the top edge of the paper and the center of the gutter meet.

You might, however, prefer a different zero point. For example, many users like to have the zero point at the intersection of the top and left margins of the current page; with this setting, measurements from the zero point will show distances within the usable area of the page that's being created. You might even want to place the zero point temporarily at the top corner of a graphic so you can easily drag the image to make it an exact size.

You can change the zero point at any time, even in the midst of working on a document. You can also lock the zero point so it can't be changed accidentally. Here's how:

1. Place the pointer on the small box containing dotted lines forming crosshairs, located at the intersection of the two rulers (see Figure 7.2).

2. Hold down the left mouse button and drag. You'll see crosshairs representing the zero point move across the page in the direction you drag. Drag horizontally and/or vertically until the zeros on the rulers have moved to where you want them.

3. Release the mouse button.

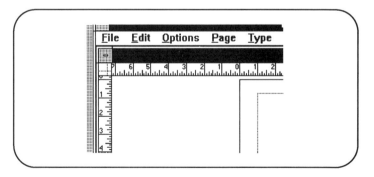

Figure 7.2: The default zero point, showing zero point crosshairs at the intersection of the rulers

4. If you want to lock the zero point in its new position, pull down the **Options** menu and select **Zero lock**. A checkmark will appear beside that option on the menu. (To unlock the zero point later so you can change it again, simply reselect the command.)

Using Ruler Guides

Remember that you use the **Page setup** command to specify the margins for your publication (see Step 3).

Next you'll want to create ruler guides. *Ruler guides* are nonprinting lines you can drag from the horizontal and/or vertical rulers to help you position elements of your layout. You can have up to 40 ruler guides in a publication, established on your master pages and/or on individual pages. To avoid clutter on your pages, it's a good idea to use only as many ruler guides as you need and to eliminate individual guides as soon as they've accomplished their purpose. One reason you might want a ruler guide on a master page would be to help you position a header or footer or to add page numbers.

Add a ruler guide like this:

1. Place the pointer on either ruler, hold down the left mouse button, and drag the pointer onto your page. A line will appear that is parallel to the ruler; this is a *ruler guide.*

2. Drag the line until it's where you want it, measuring by the point at which it touches the other ruler. While you drag, the line will be bracketed by small arrows pointing away from the line at right angles to it.

3. Release the mouse button. The guide will remain in that position.

To remove a ruler guide, just drag it off of the page.

Figure 7.3 shows a ruler guide that has been used to establish the *baseline* for a header.

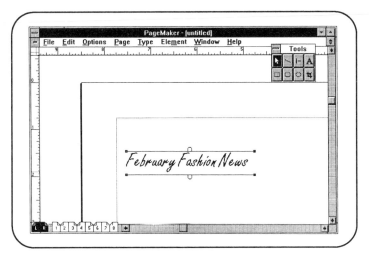

Figure 7.3: A header, with text block resting on a ruler guide

Specifying Columns

Until you specify the number of columns you want in your publication, it's assumed that each page consists of just one column that extends from its left margin to its right margin. You can have up to 20 columns; each column must be at least 1 *pica* wide. (A pica is 12 points or 1/6 of an inch.)

You set up your columns by using the **Column guides** dialog box. Here's the procedure:

1. Pull down the **Options** menu and select the **Column guides...** command. You'll see the dialog box shown in Figure 7.4.

2. If you're working with facing pages and want left and right pages to have different column settings, click the box that reads **Set left and right pages separately**. (This box appears only if you've previously selected the **Facing pages** option from the **Page setup** dialog box.) You'll then be presented with separate text boxes for specifying columns for left and right pages.

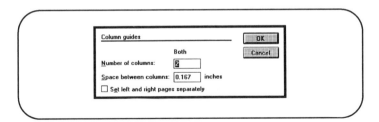

Figure 7.4: The Column guides dialog box

3. Now enter the figures you want in the boxes labeled **Number of columns** and **Space between columns**. If you want to use a different measuring system for column spacing than you've chosen in the **Preferences** dialog box, you can do so; just enter a one-letter abbreviation along with the number. You can type **i** for **inches, m** for **millimeters, c** for **ciceros,** or **p** for **picas** after the number; however, to indicate **points** as the unit of measurement, you type **p** *before* the number.

4. Click **OK**. The dialog box will close, and PageMaker will draw lines that are *column guides* for the columns you've specified on your master page(s). (You can set up a different column arrangement on any individual page by invoking the **Column guides...** command from that page instead of from the master page.)

5. You can add *rules* (vertical printed lines) between columns by using the **perpendicular-line** tool. (See the explanation of tools in Step 4.)

All columns on a page are initially drawn as equal in width. If you want to change the width of any column, just drag one of its column guides horizontally until it has the width you want.

To lock the positions of both the ruler and column guides so they can't be moved accidentally, pull down the **Options** menu and select the **Lock guides** command. Select the same command again to unlock the guides.

To hide guides (or display them again), pull down the **Options** menu and select the **Guides** command.

To align objects exactly with guides, pull down the **Options** menu and select the **Snap to guides** command. Objects near guides will position themselves exactly on the guides. This is the default—the command displays a checkmark. If you want to position objects near but not on the guides, select the active **Snap to guides** command; the checkmark will disappear, and objects will no longer snap to the guides. You can change the status of this command as often as you like in creating a publication, providing you with complete positioning flexibility.

Changing or Removing Master Items on Regular Pages

You can change master guides on any individual page (except when the **Lock guides** command is active); just select the page you want to change and drag the guides into a new position. This action will not effect the location of the master guides on other pages of your publication.

You can also eliminate all of the master-page items from any page. Merely pull down the **Page** menu and select the **Display master items** command.

Why would you want to reposition master guides or eliminate the master-page items? A typical situation would be when you have established master pages for a two-column newsletter, including rules to divide the columns. However, on one page you want to display a full-page illustration. Obviously, you won't want vertical lines intended to separate columns running through the illustration.

Master pages are made to help you—not restrict you.

Step 8
Working with Page Numbers

When you're creating any PageMaker document more than one page in length, you'll probably want to include page numbers. You can generate these automatically—provided you set up the numbering procedure on your master pages.

Before you establish page numbers, be sure you have clicked either the **L** or **R** icon so that you're working on a master page, not one of the regular pages of your document. Automatic page numbering works only when you set it up on master pages.

Specifying How You Want Pages Numbered

By default, PageMaker uses standard Arabic numeral page numbering. In other words, your pages will be numbered simply *1, 2, 3,* and so on. However, you may prefer to number your document with capital Roman numerals (*I, II, III*), lowercase Roman numerals (*i, ii, iii*), capital alphabetic characters (*A, B, C*), or lowercase alphabetic characters (*a, b, c*).

To change the default numbering system, follow this routine:

1. Pull down the **File** menu and select the **Page setup...** command. The **Page setup** dialog box will appear.

2. In the **Page setup** dialog box, click the button labeled **Numbers...**. The **Page numbering** dialog box will appear.

3. Click the button for the numbering system you prefer (see Figure 8.1).

4. Click **OK** twice to return to your publication.

For long reports or nonfiction books, you may want to use a composite numbering system; for example, the pages of Chapter 2 might be numbered *2.1, 2.2, 2.3,* etc. You'll learn how to set this up on your master page shortly. However, if you want to generate a table of contents and/or an index for your publication, you must provide for composite numbers in the **Page numbering** dialog box.

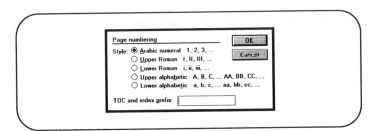

Figure 8.1: The Page numbering dialog box

You'll note that there is a rectangle at the bottom of this dialog box that's labeled **TOC and index prefix:**. Here you must type the *prefix* to be used for your page numbers, so it will be recognized and included in the table of contents and index. For example, for a numbering system for Chapter 2, wherein the first page of the chapter will be numbered *2.1,* you would type "2." in the box; these characters would constitute the prefix for any page number in that chapter. (You actually create a table of contents or index by using the **Create TOC...** or **Create Index...** commands on the **Options** menu.)

Placing Page Numbers on Your Master Pages

Page numbers can be part of a header or footer that includes other information, such as the name of the publication or chapter, and graphic elements, such as a company logo or a decorative symbol. On the other hand, you can number your pages in a separate header or footer containing no other elements. You may want to show page numbers only on right-hand pages, with the name of the document in the same position on the left-hand pages. If you number every page, you may want to center the page numbers. Or, you might prefer to have them displayed near the outside margin of each page—in other words, in one position on left-hand pages and in another position on right-hand pages.

These are all design considerations. Using PageMaker, you can select any of these options.

Follow this procedure to set up your page numbers:

1. Click on the **L** or **R** icon at the bottom of your screen to select the master page where the numbers are to appear.

2. Place the pointer on the horizontal ruler and drag down to create a ruler guide for the header or footer that will contain the page numbers.

3. Pull down the **Type** menu and select the typeface and point size you want to use.

4. Click the **text** tool to select it, and drag it across the approximate area where you want the header or footer, to form a rectangle to enclose the text. (You won't see the rectangle after you release the mouse button, but the text boundaries will have been defined.)

5. Type the text, including a title or other information if you wish. At the point where you want the page number, you may want to type the word *Page* to precede the number. If you want to generate composite numbers (such as *2.1*), type the prefix "2." (Be sure to include the period after the number.)

6. Then, place the cursor where you want the actual number to appear that is to change automatically from page to page. (In the *2.1* example, this position would be immediately after the decimal point.) Press **Ctrl-Shift-3**. The characters *LM* (on a left-hand master page) or *RM* (on a right-hand master page) will appear. In other words, using the same example, you would see the characters *2.LM* on the screen for a left-hand master page representing Chapter 2. On the regular pages of the publication, the *LM* would be replaced by the actual page number.

7. Click the **pointer** tool to end text entry, and then click the text block to select it. Drag the text block as necessary to line it up perfectly on the header or footer ruler guide you've created. (If you have the **Snap to guides** command active (explained in Step 7), the text block will automatically align itself to the guide when you get its baseline close to the ruler guide.)

Figure 8.2 shows a right-hand master page, with the page-numbering procedure set up on a header ruler guide.

If you want to add a graphic to your header or footer, use the **Place**... command from the **File** menu (see Step 5) to import the graphic into your publication. Then size the image and drag it onto the header or footer ruler guide for the master page.

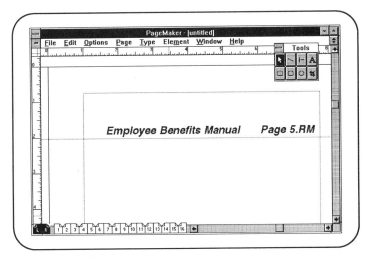

Figure 8.2: Setting up automatic page numbering

Step 9
Placing & Flowing Text

So far you've learned how to create small text blocks right on your pages. However, most desktop publishing involves larger quantities of text; you may want to import this text from a document created in a word-processing program, type the text in Page-Maker's Story editor (explained in Step 11), paste it in by way of the clipboard from another Windows application such as a spreadsheet or database program, or convert it from an ASCII file received by modem.

Regardless of the source of the text, PageMaker can arrange it into columns and thread a story from column to column automatically. You can also choose to direct the flow manually—starting a story on page 1 of a newsletter, for example, and continuing it on page 3. (You can also flow text around graphics. This is covered in Step 10.)

As explained in Step 4, text blocks have boundaries with square block handles you can drag to reshape a block. They also have windowshade handles on the top and bottom that you can use to control the flow of text from column to column and page to page.

Making Text Autoflow

The easiest way to work with text blocks is to make the **Autoflow** command active before you import the text. When this command is selected, text will flow automatically from column to column and page to page. If needed, new pages will even be added to your publication automatically to accommodate the entire document.

This is how you activate and deactivate Autoflow:

1. Pull down the **Options** menu and select the **Autoflow** command (as shown in Figure 9.1). A checkmark will appear beside the command, indicating that it is now active.

2. To deactivate Autoflow, pull down the **Options** menu again and select the **Autoflow** command again. The checkmark beside the command will disappear, indicating that it has been deactivated.

PageMaker will automatically deactivate Autoflow if you place a text block by dragging it, place text onto the pasteboard instead of onto a page, or place text from the middle of an existing story.

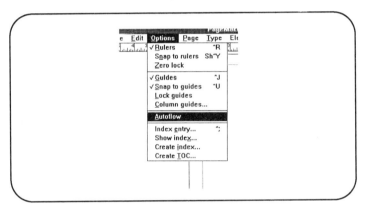

Figure 9.1: Selecting the Autoflow command

Importing Text

Of course, before you can position text in a publication, you must have that text available. The most frequently used method of importing text is through the **Place...** command (explained in Step 5 in relation to graphic files). Here is the procedure to follow:

*Importing
text with
the Place...
command*

1. Pull down the **File** menu and select the **Place...** command. You'll see the **Place file** dialog box.

2. Select the text file you want to import by highlighting it in the list box of the dialog box. If you need to change the active drive or directory to locate the file, scroll the **Files/ Directories** list box until you see the name of the directory or drive you want, and then double-click it. Then double-click again to select the file name and import it. PageMaker

will recognize most popular word-processing formats and convert them automatically.

3. If you want to select an importation option, click only once on the file name, and then pick the manner in which you want the file imported by clicking one of the buttons in the **Place:** section of the dialog box. The options are as follows: **As new story**, which is the default (shown in Figure 9.2); **Replacing entire story**, which replaces all of an existing story with the new file; and **Inserting text**, which inserts the text into an existing story at the point where you place the pointer. If you've previously selected existing text (by highlighting it before issuing the **Place...** command), this last option will read **Replacing selected text**.

4. In the **Options** area of the dialog box, you can click boxes to select or deselect three options. **Retain format** preserves the formatting established in the application in which the text was created, if possible (even typefaces chosen are retained from other applications such as Word for Windows); if this box is unchecked, the current Page-Maker default formatting will be used. **Convert quotes**, if selected, automatically changes ordinary identical quotation marks into distinct opening and closing quotation marks such as those normally seen in books and magazines.

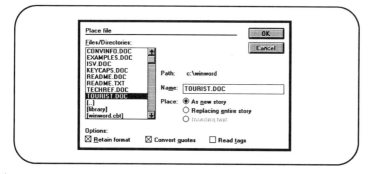

Figure 9.2: The Place file dialog box, showing text importing options

Read tags is the only one of the three options that is not selected by default; it causes PageMaker to look for style-name tags you can insert into files from word processors that don't have defined styles. The tags must be enclosed in angle brackets (for example, *<Headline>*) and to be recognized, they must be currently defined PageMaker styles.

5. If you made changes in the dialog box instead of double-clicking the file name, click **OK** to proceed with importing the text file. The pointer will now assume the shape of the upper left corner of a document. There are three possible variations on this shape: the pointer will show simulated text if Autoflow is not selected, it will show a curved path ending in an arrow if Autoflow is selected, or it will show a dotted path ending in an arrow if you hold down the **Shift** key during placement. This last variation makes Autoflow placement semiautomatic, with automatic flow only to the bottom of the column where placement begins.

6. Place the pointer at the spot where you want the text file to start, and click the left mouse button (holding down the **Shift** key if you want semiautomatic placement). The text will flow into the appropriate columns. You can interrupt the text flow by clicking the mouse button again.

You can also import text from the Story Editor (see Step 11), or from other PageMaker documents or Windows applications through the clipboard.

This is the procedure for using the clipboard:

Importing text through the clipboard

1. Drag across the text in the other Windows file to select it.

2. Pull down the **Edit** menu and select **Copy** to copy the text to the clipboard, or select **Cut** to remove the text from the other Windows file for use in PageMaker.

3. Activate PageMaker (if it's not already loaded) and select the page where you want the text inserted.

4. Place the pointer where you want the text inserted and click the left mouse button.

5. Pull down the PageMaker **Edit** menu and select **Paste**. The text will now appear on your PageMaker page.

Flowing Text

As already mentioned, you can select Autoflow and have your text flow automatically until the entire file has been placed.

However, you can control placement of portions of a text file very precisely. This is done by dragging text blocks to change their position, dragging their square handles to reshape them, or by pulling the windowshade handles to control the flow.

Every text block has windowshade handles centered at the top and bottom of the block. However, although the text itself is always visible, the windowshade handles are displayed only if you've clicked the block to select it.

Explanation of windowshade handles

The appearance of windowshades tells you a lot about the text contained in the block. If a top or bottom handle is empty, there is no text beyond that point. Therefore, an empty top windowshade handle indicates the beginning of the story, and an empty bottom windowshade handle marks the end of the story.

A plus sign (+) in the top handle means that at least one text block from the same story exists at some preceding location (see Figure 9.3). A plus sign in the bottom handle means that at least one text block from that story follows, further on in the publication.

A down arrow can appear in the bottom windowshade handle only. This signifies that there is text in the block that has not been placed yet. If you print a publication with a text block that exhibits a down arrow in a windowshade, of course the windowshade itself will not print. Neither will any text that is not visible on the screen (when the block is displayed in a large enough size so that the text is not greeked).

Handling unplaced text

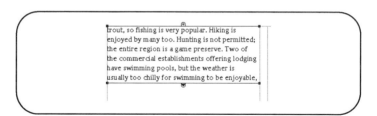

trout, so fishing is very popular. Hiking is
enjoyed by many too. Hunting is not permitted;
the entire region is a game preserve. Two of
the commercial establishments offering lodging
have swimming pools, but the weather is
usually too chilly for swimming to be enjoyable,

Figure 9.3: A text block with plus and down-arrow windowshades

Here's how to handle unplaced text:

1. To place the remaining text at the same location (adding it to the text that is already visible), simply pull down the windowshade.

2. If there is no room for the remaining text at that location, or if you want to place the remaining text elsewhere in the publication, click the windowshade handle containing the down arrow. This action will create an additional text block (containing the unplaced text) which can be dragged to a new location.

Adjusting
text blocks

PageMaker keeps track of the location of all of the text in a story, regardless of how many blocks have been created to contain portions of it. For example, after you've placed the text, if you decide you want to display more of the story in a particular column and pull down the bottom windowshade to accomplish this, the contents of the remaining text blocks will be adjusted automatically, with the final block being shortened.

On the other hand, if you shorten a block, none of the later blocks will change in size automatically; the final block will display a down arrow, indicating that you can either pull down the bottom windowshade to display the extra text at that point, or click the windowshade to create one more text block for use elsewhere.

Unthreading
and
rethreading
text

If you don't want the portions of a story to remain connected (perhaps so you can format them separately), you can unthread a text block like this:

1. Select the text block with the pointer.
2. Pull down the **Edit** menu and select **Cut**.
3. With nothing selected on the page, pull down the **Edit** menu again and select **Paste**. The text block will remain in its original position, but will no longer be threaded automatically as part of the story.

You can also rethread a text block. This is the procedure:

1. Select the unthreaded text block.
2. Pull down the **Edit** menu and select **Cut**.

3. Click the **text** tool and click an insertion point in a text block where you want to rethread the text back into the story.
4. Pull down the **Edit** menu and select **Paste**. The text will disappear from its previous location and will be threaded back into the story.

Step 10

Integrating Graphics with Text

Few graphic images are included in a publication without some relationship to text in that publication. When text flows around a graphic without any relationship, the graphic is classified as *independent*. On the other hand, you can also make a graphic function as part of a text story, so that it acts like a paragraph and moves in concert with the text portions of the story, maintaining its same position in relation to the paragraphs of text that precede or follow it. In fact, you can even place a graphic so that it functions as a separate text block, complete with its own windowshades. A graphic included as part of a text story is referred to as an *inline* graphic.

So far, in earlier Steps, you've dealt with graphic images as *independent* graphics. In this Step, you'll learn how to integrate both independent and inline graphics with text.

Integrating Independent Graphics

After the graphic has been added to the publication with the **Place...** command, you can easily specify how you want it to interrelate with text by using the **Text wrap...** command. You can also add and drag handles to customize the boundaries of the graphic and the manner in which text will wrap around it.

Use this technique to control the automatic integration of text with an independent graphic:

1. Click the graphic to select it.

2. Pull down the **Element** menu and select the **Text wrap...** command. You'll see the **Text wrap** dialog box.

3. Click a **Wrap option** icon to specify whether or not you want text to wrap around the graphic. The first icon option (on the left) makes text flow over the graphic; in other words, the graphic will remain in the background behind

the text. The second (or middle) option creates a rectangular graphic boundary around which the text can flow. If you have already customized the boundaries of the graphic (discussed later in this Step), the third icon will be selected automatically; otherwise, this icon will be grayed out and unavailable for selection. You can cancel out any custom boundary changes by clicking the middle icon to return the boundaries to a rectangular shape.

4. Next, click one of three **Text flow** icons to choose how you want the text to flow around the graphic. The first option is the **Column-break** icon, which makes PageMaker stop flowing text in a column when the graphic is encountered and then makes it continue the flow at the top of the next column. The second option is the **Jump-over** icon, which stops text flow when the graphic is reached in the column and then continues it below the graphic in the same column. The third and final option is the **Wrap-all-sides** icon, which makes text flow around the icon on all sides (selected in Figure 10.1).

5. If you want to change the default standoff of .167 inches around a rectangular graphic (to move the text closer or further away from the image), type a new number

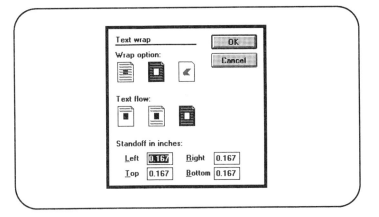

Figure 10.1: The Text wrap dialog box

(in inches decimal) in one or more of the four **Standoff in inches** boxes: **Left, Right, Top,** and **Bottom.**

Customizing Graphic Boundaries

If you're using a graphic image that is not rectangular in shape and you want to wrap text around it, you can drag portions of the image's boundaries to reflect its actual contours.

Use this technique:

1. Click the image to select it, and then pull down the **Element** menu.

2. Select the **Text wrap...** command. The **Text wrap** dialog box will appear.

3. Click the middle icon in the **Wrap option** area of the dialog box—the one that creates a rectangular graphic boundary. By default, selecting this icon will also cause the right-hand **Text flow** option below to be selected—the **Wrap-all-sides** icon. The boundary that will appear around the graphic consists of a rectangle composed of dashes, with a small handle at each of its four corners.

4. To extend or contract the boundary at one of the four corners where handles are displayed, drag the handle to reshape the boundary pattern.

5. If you wish to reshape a boundary at a point where no handle exists, click the boundary at that location; a new handle will be added. Then drag the new handle to adjust the boundary shape (see Figure 10.2).

6. To remove a handle, drag it over an adjacent handle.

Don't confuse the handles of the broken-line graphic boundary with the six larger handles surrounding the boundary; these larger handles appear any time you select a graphic. Dragging one of the large handles will not customize the graphic boundary, but will only resize the graphic! (See Step 5.)

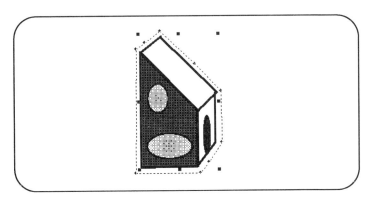

Figure 10.2: An irregular graphic with boundaries reshaped for proper text flow

Creating Inline Graphics

To import a graphic and make it part of a text story (an inline graphic), follow this procedure:

1. Select the **text** tool, and click or drag to create an insertion point. If you use the drag technique to create a rectangle to receive the graphic, the graphic will become a separate text box with its own windowshades; just be sure you make the rectangle large enough to display the entire image.

2. Pull down the **File** menu and select the **Place...** command. The **Place document** dialog box will appear.

3. In the **Place document** dialog box, select the graphic file to be imported and click the button labeled **As inline graphic**.

4. Click **OK**. The graphic will then appear at the insertion point as an inline graphic (see Figure 10.3).

You can now treat the graphic as text, except that you cannot apply style attributes such as boldface to it. Also you cannot drag the graphic to the left or right within the column. However, you can crop it or resize it to make it occupy a desired area.

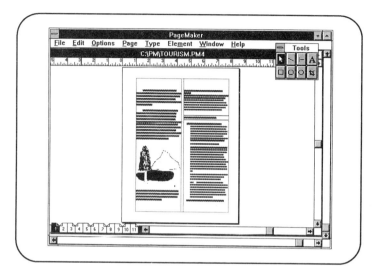

Figure 10.3: An inline graphic

Converting Graphics
to and from Independent Status

Here's how to convert an independent graphic into an inline graphic:

1. Select the graphic.
2. Pull down the **Edit** menu and select the **Cut** command.
3. Select the **text** tool and select an insertion point.
4. Pull down the **Edit** menu and select **Paste**. The graphic will now be an inline part of a text block.

To convert an inline graphic to an independent graphic:

1. Select **pointer** tool, and then the graphic.
2. Pull down the **Edit** menu and select the **Cut** command.

3.   Pull down the **Edit** menu again and select the **Paste** command.

The graphic is now independent and can be moved without reference to the text story from which it was cut.

Step 11
Editing Text

In earlier Steps you worked with text displayed as part of a publication; usually, both text and graphics were shown in a close approximation of how they would look when printed. PageMaker calls this method of display *layout view.* In earlier versions of the program, this was the only view available.

However, now you can choose to display text in *story view.* This view shows text only—and only in one size. This is a much faster environment for both text editing and, in fact, for creating text—if you prefer to type stories within PageMaker rather than importing them from another source, such as a word-processing program. Story view itself is actually a mini word-processing program.

Story view offers three other major advantages:

- You can open multiple story windows and transfer text between them.

- You get search-and-replace capabilities, even extending to such features as the typeface used, point size, or the style of a paragraph.

- You can check the spelling of text, with a 100,000-word dictionary.

Entering Story View

You can enter story view from layout view to edit a story in several ways:

- Triple-click a text block in a story.

- Select the text block, pull down the **File** menu, and select **Edit story**. (See Figure 11.1.)

- Select the text block and press **Ctrl-E**.

- Select the **text** tool, click an insertion point in a text block, pull down the **File** menu, and select **Edit story**.

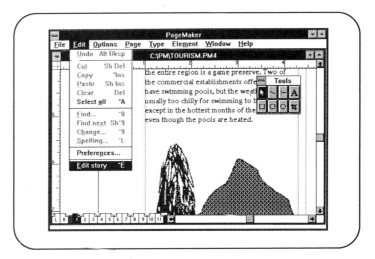

Figure 11.1: Selecting Edit story from the Edit menu

- Select the **text** tool, click an insertion point in a text block, and press **Ctrl-E**.

To create a *new* story (where you intend to type all of the text in story view), just pull down the **Edit** menu and select **Edit story**, or press **Ctrl-E** *when no text is selected and there is no active insertion point in a text block.* The resulting text will be a new story.

Editing a Story

When you select **Edit story** while an existing story is active in layout view, you will enter story view with that story displayed for editing in a small vertical window at the left of your screen. It will be shown in the typeface and size selected in the **Preferences** dialog box. (See Step 7.) Small markers within the text will be the only indication of the presence of inline graphics, page numbers, or index entries.

If you plan to do more than make minor changes in an existing story, click the Windows Maximize button (the up arrow in the upper right corner of the window) to enlarge the story-view window to a full-screen display. Then you can look at more of the text at once—as much as you would see in a word processor.

There is no toolbox in story view (it is not needed here), and the window is named with the first few words of the story (instead of a file name). You will not see text flowed into columns nor will you see the letter and word spacing that would be applied in layout view. In addition, the menus will be slightly different, as shown in Figure 11.2.

In story view you can edit text much as you would in most graphic-based word processors:

- To insert new text, click to establish the insertion point. The pointer will assume the shape of an I-beam. Type the material you wish to add. Existing text will shift to the right to make room.

- To delete existing text, drag over the text you want to remove, highlighting and selecting it, and then press the

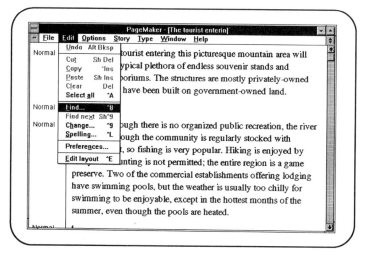

Figure 11.2: The story view of a document, with the Find... command selected

Delete key. (There is an alternate method of deletion: after selecting the text, pull down the **Edit** menu and choose **Clear**.)

- To move or copy existing text, drag to select the text, pull down the **Edit** menu and choose **Cut** or **Copy**, click where you want the highlighted text to reappear, and then pull down the **Edit** menu again and choose **Paste**. (Here are shortcuts for these commands: **Cut**, *Shift-Delete;* **Copy**, *Ctrl-Insert;* **Paste**, *Shift-Insert.*)

- To change the appearance of existing text, drag to select the text, and then apply whatever menu options you wish, such as changing to a new typeface, changing a normal font to boldface, changing the color of text, and so on. Style changes such as boldface will be shown on the screen. However, color and typeface changes will be displayed only when you return to layout view. To change an attribute throughout a story, or in a long story, use the **Change...** command (explained in Step 12). Story view can display only *screen* fonts that have been installed in Windows. If you have a typeface installed that has only a printer font, you can select it from the **Font** menu and print it; however, it will not be displayed correctly in story view.

Leaving Story View

You can change to layout view without closing the story-view window in these ways:

- If you can see a portion of the publication window, click it to activate it.

- If you can't see the publication window, pull down the **Window** menu and click the file name of the publication.

- Pull down the **Edit** menu, and choose **Edit layout**. This command will appear in the same position on this menu that is occupied by the **Edit story** command when you're in layout view.

To *close* story view and return to layout view, pull down the **Story** menu and choose **Close story.** (A shortcut for this command is to press **Shift-Ctrl-E.**)

Using any of these methods to return to layout view, you will see that any changes you have made in story view have been incorporated automatically into the story in layout view.

If you close the story window by selecting **Close** from the **File** menu instead of **Close story** from the **Story** menu, you will close the publication, including all open windows. However, if you've made changes, you'll be asked if you want to save them.

Placing a New Story

If you have created a new story in story view, it will not be placed in your publication automatically. However, if you try to close the story window without having placed it, you will see a small dialog box, where you'll be asked to place the story, discard it, or cancel the **Close story** command.

If you choose **Place** from this dialog box, or pull down the **File** menu and choose the **Place** command, the pointer will assume the shape of a loaded text icon. Place the pointer at the point in the publication where you want the story to appear, and click; the new story will now become a part of the publication and will be printed along with the rest of it.

The **Place** command in story view is not the same as the **Place...** command in layout view. In layout view, you use the command to import a file from disk into your current publication. In story view, you use the command only to insert a new story you've just typed.

Step 12
Finding & Changing Text

Story view (see Step 11) provides powerful capabilities for locating and replacing both text and attributes such as the occurrences of a particular typeface or a certain paragraph style in the currently selected story or in all stories in the publication. First you'll learn how to locate text.

Searching for Specific Text

To locate specific text, use the **Find...** command. Here's how:

1. Select the story, or drag to select part of a story, and switch to story view, by pressing Ctrl-E (the shortcut for the **Edit Story** command).

2. Pull down the **Edit** menu and choose the **Find...** command. (You can also use the shortcut, **Ctrl-8.**) A small dialog box for this command will appear. (See Figure 12.1.)

3. If you want to find instances of a particular word or phrase, type the text to be found in the **Find what** box.

4. If you want the *case* (the same combination of capital and lowercase characters) to be matched, click the box labeled **Match case.**

5. If you want the search to involve whole words only, click the box labeled **Whole word.**

6. To limit the search to a selected portion of a story, click the button labeled **Selected text.**

7. To limit the search to the current story (the default), leave the **Current story** button selected.

8. To search *all* stories in the publication, click the button labeled **All stories.**

9. Finally, click the large **Find** button. The program will highlight the first occurrence of the text specified. The **Find**

button will then change to read **Find next**. (If the text is
not found, a small message box will appear, stating **Search
complete**; you then click **OK** to leave the **Find** command
and return to the story.)

10. Click the **Find next** button to search for the next occurrence of the text specified.

11. Double-click the close box at any point to terminate the
search.

Figure 12.1: The Find dialog box

Searching for Attributes

In addition to using the **Find...** command for locating text, you
can fine-tune your text search to bring up a word, for example,
only when it appears in italics, or only when it appears in the Cooper Black typeface. You can also ignore specific text entirely and
retrieve all text used as headings, or all text in an 18-point size,
and so on.

Click the **Attributes...** button in the **Find** dialog box; this action
will display a subsidiary dialog box called **Find attributes.** You
can enter search specifications here, or in combination with the
main **Find** dialog box, to locate almost any specific text/attribute
combination.

Here are the options for **Find attributes:**

- **Para style** means *paragraph style* and is set by default to
  read **Any**. Click the drop-down menu, and you'll see any
  currently defined paragraph styles as choices, including

Body text, **Caption**, and **Headline**. Click any style to incorporate it in your search.

- **Font** is where you can search for specific typefaces. Again, the default is **Any**; the drop-down menu will display a list of all of the typefaces installed in your copy of Windows. Click any name to select it.

- **Size** refers to the *point size*. The default is **Any**. You can change this criterion by clicking one of the sizes shown in the drop-down menu or by typing some other size in the box.

- **Type style** displays **Any** by default, but can be changed by clicking boxes. You can search for **Normal** or combinations of the following: **Bold**, **Italic**, **Underline**, **Strikethru**, or **Reverse** (white type on a black background).

Click **OK** when you've finished making selections on this submenu, or click **Cancel** to return to the Find dialog box without making or changing selections.

Changing Text and Attributes

If you pull down the **Edit** menu and pick **Change...** instead of **Find...**, you'll see a dialog box almost identical to the one brought up with the **Find...** command. (The shortcut for pulling down the **Edit** menu, and then choosing **Change...** is Ctrl-9.) The only difference is that below the **Find what** box, you'll see a **Change to** box. As you might imagine, this added box lets you replace text you've typed in the top box with new text.

There are more options to the right of the **Change to** box. In addition to **Find** and **Attributes...** buttons, there are buttons with these names and functions:

- **Change** replaces text typed in the **Find what** box with text typed in the **Change to** box. After the first replacement, you'll then see a new button labeled **Find next** (instead of the **Find** button); click this button to proceed to the next occurrence of the text to be found and changed.

- **Change & find** replaces located text with the revised text, and then automatically looks for the next occurrence.

- **Change all** automatically finds and replaces all occurrences of the text to be located, without any further action on your part. If no such text is found, you'll see an alert message.

When you use the **Change...** command, you'll discover that clicking the **Attributes...** button will display the **Attributes** dialog box. At the left side of this box, you'll see the same features available in the **Find attributes** dialog box connected with the **Find** command; these options are headed with the word *Find.* However, to the right of this list, the same features are shown again, under the heading **Change** (see Figure 12.2). All you have to do is enter existing attributes in the left series of boxes, and the changes you want in the boxes in the right series of boxes.

For example, in Figure 12.2 a style change is being made in a publication, without any text change (although you could change the text as well). All headings that are currently displayed in the Bodoni Poster typeface in 24 pt. bold will be replaced by the Futura Condensed typeface in 30 pt. bold.

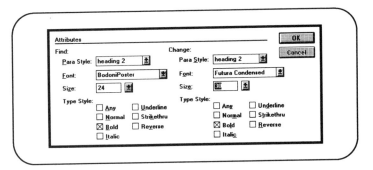

Figure 12.2: Changing attributes with the Change... command

Step 13
Checking Spelling

 15

From story view (explained in Step 11), you can check the spelling of selected text, the current story (the default), or all stories in your current publication.

Follow this procedure:

1. Pull down the **Edit** menu and click the **Spelling...** command. The **Spelling** dialog box will appear.

2. To check the spelling of all of the words in the current story, just click the **Start** button.

3. To check only **Selected text** or to check **All stories,** click the appropriate button, and then click **Start.** After you press **Start,** the same dialog box remains on the screen, but the spellchecker will highlight a word it does not recognize and display it in the **Change to** box.

4. To change a word displayed in the dialog box as an **Unknown word,** either click one of the suggested correctly spelled words in the list box as a replacement, or type a correction in the text box labeled **Change to:** and click the **Replace** button.

5. To add a word to or remove a word from the user dictionary, click the **Add...** button. A smaller dialog box will appear, where you can type the word. If you have already stopped on a word in the previous dialog box, you don't need to type in the word; it will automatically appear in the **Word** box of the **Add word to user dictionary** dialog box. If you're adding a word, you can click the **As all lowercase** button to have PageMaker accept any combination of lowercase and capital letters as a correct spelling; if you click the **Exactly as typed** button, the program will flag any instances of the word with different capitalization. Click **OK** to add the word to the dictionary, **Remove** to remove

the word, or **Cancel** to return to the previous dialog box.

6. If a flagged word is correctly spelled, but you don't want to add it to the dictionary, click the **Ignore** button; it appears in place of the **Start** button after the spellcheck begins.

7. To leave the **Spelling** dialog box after you see the message *Spelling check complete,* double-click the close box.

If you have more than one dictionary installed, you can select the one you want to use before starting a spellcheck.

This is the procedure:

Changing diction-aries

1. Pull down the **Type** menu and select **Paragraph...** (shortcut: press **Ctrl-M**).

2. Click the **Dictionary** box to activate the drop-down menu showing installed dictionaries.

3. Click the name of the dictionary you want, and then click **OK** to return to the story view window.

Figure 13.1 shows a spellcheck in progress. PageMaker has

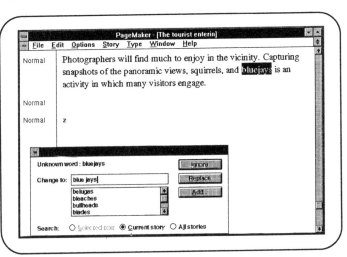

Figure 13.1: A spellcheck in progress

flagged the word *bluejays,* which it does not recognize. The word has been retyped as two words (*blue jays*). At this point, it's only necessary to click the **Replace** button to continue with the spellcheck.

Step 14

Setting Indents & Tab Stops

You can set paragraph indentations and tab stops very precisely in PageMaker. You can specify special configurations such as *hanging indents* (where the first line of a paragraph is indented less than the remaining lines) and tab stops that will align numbers to decimal points.

When and where your changes take effect will depend upon the status of your publication at the time. Here are the rules:

- To change indent and/or tab defaults for all text you subsequently add to the current publication, make the changes with the **pointer** tool active (and no text selected).

- To change indents and/or tabs only for an existing paragraph, use the **text** tool to click within the paragraph before you make the changes.

- To change indents and/or tabs in an entire story or part of a story, use the **text** tool to drag and select the text before you make the changes.

The default Indents/tabs dialog box is shown in Figure 14.1. To display this dialog box, follow this procedure:

1. Select text, as explained above, if you want to make setting changes only in a specific story or part of a story, rather than changing the defaults for the publication.

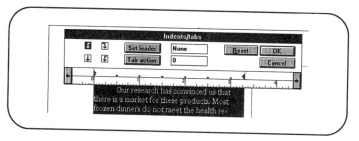

Displaying the Indents/ tabs dialog box

Figure 14.1: The Indents/tabs dialog box with default settings

2. Pull down the **Type** menu and choose the **Indents/tabs** command. (As an alternative shortcut, you can simply press **Ctrl-I**.)

Setting the Ruler and Indents

You'll note that this dialog box includes a ruler, with the zero point located at its left end; this is the point from which indentation and tab-stop settings will be measured. If no text is selected when the box is displayed, the zero point will be established at the left margin of the page. If text in a column is selected and the left guide for the column is visible, the zero point will be at the left boundary of the column.

You can move the zero point by clicking the left- or right-pointing arrows at the ends of the ruler.

Now look closely just above the zero point. You'll see two small triangles, stacked one on top of the other. Use these to change line indentations. Here's how:

Changing line indents

1. If you only want to set a left indentation for the first line, drag the top triangle to the right along the ruler, to the position where you want the indent.

2. If you want a hanging indent, drag the bottom triangle to the right (the top triangle will move with it), to the point where you want the indentation for all of the lines of the paragraph except the first line. Then drag the top triangle back to the left, to the point where you want the indentation for the first line. (With a hanging indent, this point may be the left boundary of the column.)

3. To indent the right margin of the text, you must move the larger, left-facing triangle situated above the right boundary of the column (or the right margin of the page, if you haven't divided the page into columns). Drag this triangle to the left, to the point where you want the right indent.

4. If you don't want to change tab settings in addition to indents, click **OK** to return to your publication. Otherwise, use the additional procedures explained below.

Changing Tab Stops

The default tab stops are tiny triangles, with the point facing down. They are all *left-alignment* tabs, meaning that the text will appear just to the right of the tab stop and that the left side of a paragraph starting with a tab will be in alignment. This type of alignment is similar in appearance to *left justification* for a column or document and is the format most people would expect when using tabs. It's the way tabs work on most typewriters.

However, in PageMaker you have three other options. You can have tabs with *right alignment,* so that the text appears to the left of the tab, with the *right* side of a resulting paragraph forming a straight line. Another option is *center alignment;* the text is centered, spread out equally to each side from the position of the tab stop. The final choice is *decimal alignment,* used in working with numbers; decimal points are aligned at the tab stop. Four icons are used to symbolize these options: *left alignment* is an arrow with its tail pointing toward the right, *right alignment* is an arrow with its tail pointing toward the left, *center alignment* is an arrow with its tail pointing straight up, and *decimal alignment* is the same as center—except that a decimal point appears to the right of the straight arrow. (See these icons in Figure 14.2.)

Here's how to set tabs:

1. If the **Indents/tabs** dialog box is not already displayed, pull down the **Type** menu and select **Indents/tabs...** (or press **Ctrl-I**).

2. Click the icon for the kind of alignment you want for the first tab.

3. Click an existing tab or some other position on the ruler where you want the tab placed. Any existing tabs to the left

of that position will disappear. The new tab will assume the shape of the alignment icon you selected.

4. Select a different alignment icon if you wish, and then click again where you want the next tab. All default tabs between the first tab and this new tab will disappear.

5. When you have entered all of the new tabs you want, click **OK** to return to your publication.

If you don't like the changes you've made, instead of clicking **OK,** click **Reset** to return all of the tabs to their defaults. You can also click **Cancel** to discard any changes and return to your publication.

There are two other buttons in this dialog box. You can enter a tab location in the edit box next to the **Tab action** button—or click a location on the ruler—if you want to add, delete, move, or repeat a tab. Then click **Tab action** to see the drop-down menu displayed in Figure 14.2.

Here's an explanation of these **Tab action** options:

Tab action
options

• **Add tab** inserts a tab at a location you've typed in the edit box. (You can also click a spot on the ruler to enter a location in this box.)

• **Delete tab** deletes a tab at the location in the edit box.

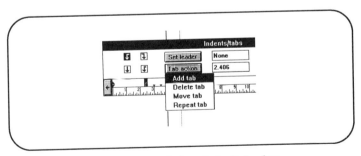

Figure 14.2: Tab setting in the Indents/tabs dialog box

- **Move tab** moves a highlighted tab from its present location to a new location you type in the edit box.

- **Repeat tab** inserts a series of tabs the same distance apart as the distance between the zero point and a highlighted tab.

The remaining button in the dialog box is labeled **Set leader**. This option has a drop-down list of *leader characters* from which you can select (or you can type your own in the text box next to the button. A *leader* is a character pattern that (if you change the default from **None**) will appear instead of spaces between tab stops. A typical table created using tab stops might display a series of dots (periods) between entries.

Step 15

Spacing Text

You have considerable control over how text is spaced in Page-Maker. If you're new to desktop publishing, you will probably find that the default settings will be satisfactory for most circumstances. However, as you become more experienced, you will want to fine-tune the spacing between lines, words, and even characters. You may simply want to fit a certain paragraph into an available area of a page without changing the type size. More often, you will want to adjust text spacing for maximum eye-appeal and readability.

Spacing Characters (Kerning)

In the old days of manual typewriters, each character took up the same amount of space on a page, regardless of its actual width. Computer typefaces that look like the output of such a typewriter are referred to as *fixed-pitch* or *monospaced*. On the other hand, typefaces that look like the text in most magazines and books—where each character occupies only as much room as it needs—are called proportional.

Most proportional typefaces contain two-character combinations that look awkward because there seems to be too much space between those characters; some examples are *Yo, Pa, Fu,* and *Ve.* You can correct this situation by moving those characters closer together, using a process called *kerning* (adjusting the spacing between two characters).

PageMaker does some automatic kerning if the proper information has been provided in computer files by the manufacturer of the typeface. However, you can easily do manual kerning of any character pair whose appearance displeases you. Here's how:

1. From the normal layout mode of PageMaker, click the **text** tool to activate it. The cursor will assume the shape of an I-beam.

How to
kern
manually

2. Place the cursor between the two characters you want to kern, and click. The cursor will become a long vertical line, as shown between the characters A and V in the top display of the capital letters AVA in Figure 15.1.

3. Press **Ctrl-+** (the **Ctrl** key simultaneously with the **plus sign** on your number keypad) to move the characters further apart; you may want to repeat these keystrokes once or twice until the characters are exactly where you want them. Press the **Ctrl** key and the **minus sign** on your number keypad together to move the characters closer together (the goal in this example). The bottom display of the letters *AVA* in Figure 15.1 shows the characters properly kerned, after using this keystroke combination only twicc between each of the two-letter pairs.

To move characters in smaller increments, hold down the **Ctrl** and **Shift** keys as you press either the plus or minus key. You cannot kern the first character of a line.

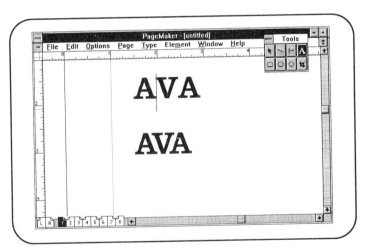

Figure 15.1: Kerning the characters AVA

Setting Automatic Spacing Standards

If you use narrow columns on your pages and want them fully *justified* (with both left and right margins straight), PageMaker must adjust the spacing between characters and words to achieve this effect.

You can tell PageMaker how you want this spacing handled, as well as the spacing between lines. This is the procedure:

1. Pull down theType menu and select the **Paragraph...** command. You'll see the **Paragraph specifications** dialog box.

2. Click the **Spacing...** button. The **Spacing attributes** dialog box will appear, with boxes where you can enter **Minimum, Desired,** and **Maximum** settings for both word and letter spacing. (See Figure 15.2.)

3. Enter new figures if you want to change the default settings (explained below).

4. Click **OK** to save changes and put them into effect, **Cancel** to leave the dialog box without saving changes, or **Reset** to return the figures to their default settings.

Word space is based on the *space band,* the space placed between words when you press the spacebar. The **Desired** setting is 100%

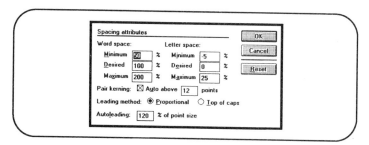

Figure 15.2: The Spacing attributes dialog box

of this measurement. Enter **Minimum** and **Maximum** percentages based on what you feel is visually acceptable. For example, with the default minimum of 50% and maximum of 200%, the space between two words will never be less than half or greater than double the normal amount. Settings in all three boxes can range between 0% and 500%. However, **Minimum** must be less than or equal to **Desired,** and **Maximum** must be greater than or equal to **Desired.**

Letter space is based on the _pen advance,_ the measurement between the left edge of a character in a particular font to the left edge of the next character. The default desired letter spacing is 0%, meaning that no spacing will be added or subtracted from this normal amount by kerning or changing the spacing between words. The default minimum is -5%, and the default maximum is 25%. You can add— or subtract (with a negative figure)—up to ±100% in the **Desired** box and up to ±200% in the **Minimum** and **Maximum** boxes.

Here are the other options on this menu:

Pair kerning is automatic above 12 points, by default, with the **Auto above** box checked. If this box is not checked, there is no automatic kerning at all. Because kerning slows down the composition of a page, you can set a size of type in points, below which there will be no kerning. Since gaps between characters are much more noticeable in large point sizes, you may be satisfied to use the default and have your screen redrawn more quickly as you work. On the other hand, if you're a perfectionist and want to kern in any size type, you may want to change the default to a lower point size.

Leading method can be set with buttons for **Proportional** or **Top of caps.** _Leading_ (pronounced "ledding") is the space between the tops of the capital letters in two successive lines and determines, therefore, how far apart your lines of text will be. **Proportional** (the default) causes the baseline of the text to be placed two-thirds of the way down the vertical area highlighted when you select a line of type (called the _slug_). The **Top of caps** choice pushes the characters higher up on the slug (as shown in Figure 15.3) and is mainly used for special effects.

Autoleading sets leading at 120% of the font size, by default. You can change this figure, or you can designate a specific leading figure in points (ignoring the font size), by selecting the **Leading** command from the **Type** menu. Reducing either the autoleading percentage or leading in points moves lines closer together.

Figure 15.4 shows a paragraph printed using the default leading and no justification. Under this paragraph, the same text is printed again, fully justified and with tighter leading (less space between the lines). As you can see, the appearance of the two samples is quite different, although the typeface and size are exactly the same.

Figure 15.3: Leading method affects vertical placement of characters on the slug

Our research has convinced us that there is a market for these products. Most frozen dinners do not meet the health requirements of those who must avoid the use of sugar. Our *GoodHealth* line would be low in calories–not an unusual feature. However, it would also contain no sugar, employing a sugar substitute to retain the taste appeal that is essential to long life for any processed food product.

Our research has convinced us that there is a market for these products. Most frozen dinners do not meet the health requirements of those who must avoid the use of sugar. Our *GoodHealth* line would be low in calories–not an unusual feature. However, it would also contain no sugar, employing a sugar substitute to retain the taste appeal that is essential to long life for any processed food product.

Figure 15.4: Text with default leading and no justification contrasted with tighter leading and full justification

Step 16
Creating & Using Text Styles

Every new PageMaker publication opens with a default text style sheet that has these styles listed: **No style, Body text, Caption, Headline, Subhead 1,** and **Subhead 2.** If you apply one of these styles to a paragraph, settings will be applied automatically for the typeface and size to be used, alignment and indentation, tab stops, hyphenation, and other features. This is a real convenience for formatting a document in a hurry. Style sheets become even more valuable when you find that you can customize them and create new ones as often as you like.

Of course, you can override elements of a style that has been applied to any paragraph. For example, you might decide to italicize a word or change an indentation.

Accessing Existing Styles

You can apply an existing style to paragraphs in two ways; here's the first one:

1. Select the **text** tool and click an insertion point in a paragraph or drag to highlight and select a group of paragraphs to which you want to apply a style.

2. Pull down the **Type** menu and select **Style.** A drop-down list of styles will appear, and you can select the one you want.

This is the second method of applying styles:

1. Repeat #1 above.

2. Pull down the **Window** menu and select **Style palette** (shortcut: press **Ctrl-Y**). A palette named **Styles** will appear just under the toolbox on your screen (unless you've moved the toolbox or turned off its display). (See Figure 16.1.) The **Styles** palette will then stay on your screen until you issue the same command again to hide it. You can

drag the palette by its title bar to any other position on your pasteboard. (Using the palette is faster than using the **Style** command on the pull-down menu because you can keep it displayed continually.)

3. Click on a style from the **Styles** palette to apply it to the selected text.

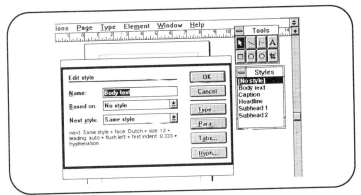

Figure 16.1: The Define styles dialog box—also showing the Styles palette under the toolbox

Editing and Creating Styles

It's easy to create new styles or edit existing ones. You can make a new style "from scratch" or base the style on an existing one by changing one or more features and giving the style a new name. For example, you might want to change all of the default styles simply because you've purchased a new typeface family that you want to substitute for the default Times Roman typeface.

If you change or create styles from the pasteboard with no publication open, you will be creating new defaults that will apply to all new publications thereafter.

Use this routine to edit or create a style:

1. Pull down the **Type** menu and select the **Define styles...** command (shortcut: press **Ctrl-3**). You'll see the **Define styles** dialog box, listing the currently defined styles. The first style name on this list will be the word **Selection** highlighted and in brackets; this is the name to pick if you want to define a new style that isn't based on any of the existing styles. Otherwise, move the highlight to an existing style to edit it or to create a variation of it.

2. To create a new style (whether based on an existing one or not), click the button labeled **New...** that is at the right side of the **Define styles** dialog box. To edit an existing style, click the **Edit...** button. In either case, your action will bring up the **Edit style** dialog box, shown in Figure 16.1; this figure also shows the **Styles** palette, displayed underneath the **Tools** palette. (Note, however, that you cannot access the **Styles** palette while you're in the **Edit Style** dialog box.)

3. If you've clicked **Edit...**, the name box in the **Edit style** dialog box will display the name of the current style; you probably won't want to change this. The default names are short and descriptive (for example: Body text or Headline). If you've clicked **New...**, the name box will be empty, with the cursor positioned within the box; type the name you want to give the new style. You can use any name you like; however, short names are easier to read, and only part of a name will be displayed if it's much longer than twenty characters (depending on the width of the characters).

4. The next text box is **Based on:** box. If you've selected a style that is not based on some other style, the box will read **No style**. If you want to base your style on a specific existing style, click the down arrow at the right of the box. A drop-down menu will appear, listing the other existing styles; click a name to select it. (When a style is based on another style, changes you make in the original style will ripple down through the derivatives. For instance, if you change a heading typeface to Cooper Black, subheads

based on this style will change typefaces too.)

5. The third and final text box is the **Next style:** box. If you want the next paragraph after the current style to be some other specific style, select the next style here. You'll probably want to choose **Same style** as the next style if you're creating a style for body copy. If you're creating a style for a subheading, on the other hand, you might want it followed by **Body text**.

6. To change a style's typeface, paragraph format, tabs and indents, or method of hyphenation, click the appropriate button in the **Edit style** dialog box: **Type...**, **Para...**, **Tabs...**, or **Hyph...**. A subsidiary dialog box will appear.

7. When you've finished making changes in one of the subsidiary dialog boxes, click **OK** to save your changes and return to the **Edit style** dialog box. Then click another button to display another subsidiary dialog box, if you want to make additional changes.

8. Click **OK** in the **Edit style** dialog box when you've finished, to save all of your changes. You'll return to the **Define styles** dialog box. If you want to change or create another style, select the style as explained in #2 earlier and repeat the procedure. Otherwise, click **OK** again to return to your document. If you've created a new style, its name will now appear on the **Style** submenu and in the **Styles** palette.

Copying Styles

You can copy the style sheet of an existing publication or template. (Templates are explained in Step 17.) This is the routine to follow:

1. Pull down the **Type** menu and select the **Define styles...** command (shortcut: press **Ctrl-3**).

2. In the **Define styles** dialog box, click the **Copy...** command. The **Copy styles** dialog box will appear, showing the names of existing publications and templates.

3. Scroll (or change to another directory) if necessary to find the file whose style sheet you want to copy. Double-click the name.

4. If you've issued these commands within an existing publication, you'll see a message asking *Copy over existing styles?* Click **OK** if you do want to replace the existing style sheet with this one; the copying process will be completed, and you can click **OK** to return to your publication. Otherwise, click **Cancel**; you'll be returned to the **Define styles** dialog box, where you can click **Cancel** again to return to your publication without changes.

You can base a new style on the formatting of an existing paragraph. Use the **text** tool to click within the paragraph or drag to highlight and select it. Then, from the **Define styles** dialog box, click **Selection** in the list box and click the **New** button. PageMaker will create a new style with the characteristics of that paragraph.

Step 17
Creating &
Using Layout Templates

15

PageMaker comes with a variety of *templates*—files with the extension .PT4 (instead of the .PM4 extension added automatically to publications). The templates are of two kinds: grid and placeholder. *Grid templates* are actually master pages with complete layout grids containing ruler and column guides and other elements appropriate for a specific kind of publication. *Placeholder templates* include master pages and style sheets (see Step 16) that you can customize, plus sample text and graphics that you can replace with your own material. Templates are provided for many purposes: newsletters, brochures, labels, business cards, catalogs, manuals, and so on.

You can also create your own templates—an especially useful function when you must produce a series of similar publications, such as weekly sales reports.

Using Existing Templates

To create a new publication based on an existing template, do the following:

1. Pull down the **File** menu and select the **Open...** command. You'll see the **Open publication** dialog box.

2. Scroll or change the directory if necessary to locate the template file you want. The file name will end with the extension .PT4.

3. Double-click the file name. This action will automatically open a copy of the template (so you'll still have the original available for future use). The copy will be an untitled publication.

4. If the template includes *placeholders* (sample text or graphics), select (highlight) an element to be replaced, and then pull down the **File** menu and choose the **Place...** command.

5. The **Place file** dialog box is now open. To replace a text placeholder, select the replacement file and click the **Replacing entire story** button; to replace a graphic placeholder, select the replacement file, click the **Replacing entire graphic** button, and then click **OK**.

6. To replace text such as a headline for which you have no replacement file ready on disk, select the **text** tool, select the placeholder text, and type the new text. Use the **Styles** palette if you want to apply different formatting, such as a change of typeface.

7. Save the new publication as a publication (rather than as a template), with a new name.

Editing a template

If you want to edit a template, open the original of the template rather than a copy, by clicking the **Original** button in the **Open publication** dialog box. Then, when you've finished editing it, save it under its original name.

Creating a New Template

You can create as many templates of your own as you like. Until you save a new template, it's simply a publication to which you can apply any column rulers, margins, typefaces, and other formatting that you desire. You can even add your own placeholder material; this can be particularly handy if someone else will have the responsibility of creating publications from the template; the other individual will then be able to see exactly what kinds of text and graphics should appear in each area.

When you're ready to save your new publication as a template, use this sequence:

1. Pull down the **File** menu and select the **Save as...** command. The **Save publication as** dialog box will appear.

2. Name the template. (PageMaker will add an extension to the file name automatically.)

3. Click the **Template** button instead of the **Publication** button. (See Figure 17.1.)

4. Click **OK**. Your new template is now complete and ready for use.

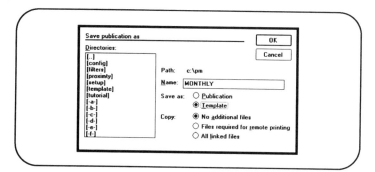

Figure 17.1: Saving a publication as a template

Step 18

Working with Color

You can apply a color to any object you create in PageMaker. However, the program treats each object as a single element; therefore, you can't apply one color to part of a graphic and another color to the rest.

Imported full-color EPS and TIFF files will not be shown with all of their colors on the screen, but can be printed correctly as part of your publications, using either a color printer or the services of a professional printshop. See Step 20, which deals with color printing.

Each PageMaker object has a name tag applied to it that keeps track of the color assigned to it. By default, the color of each object is black. Many PageMaker users who have color printing available to them add *spot color* to their publications. They change the default color of selected objects to add a touch of liveliness to pages. For example, they may print headings and borders in blue; or company policy may dictate that the corporate logo should be reproduced in a certain shade of red.

This Step will explain how you can add color to objects in your publications.

Using the Color Palette

If you want to use color, one of the first things to do is display the *color palette*. This palette resembles the tool and style palettes in appearance and convenience; it helps you make selections quickly because it's right there on your screen—not hidden in some menu structure, and you can drag it by its title bar to any location you find convenient.

To activate the color palette, simply pull down the **Window** menu and select **Color palette** (shortcut: press **Ctrl-K**). A checkmark will appear beside the selection, and the palette will appear in its default position at the right side of the screen, just below the **Styles** palette.

Initially, the **Colors** palette will show the following six items (the first three are enclosed in brackets and will always be included):

- **[Paper]** is where you can match the color of the paper you'll be using for printing.

- **[Black]** is a preset color value you can't change.

- **[Registration]** is an identification tag that always produces printing in black. You apply it to things like registration marks that are used by printshops to align color separations. Objects receiving this tag appear automatically on each *color separation*. Color separations are black and white "blueprints" of a publication, used by commercial printers to determine which areas will be printed in a particular color. You apply [Registration] as you would a color; select the object, and then select [Registration]. (Color separations are explained more fully in Step 20.)

- **Blue**, **Green**, and **Red** are basic colors provided as starting points. You can specify exact color mixes for each of these (or other colors you may add to the palette). You can also change the name shown for a color. (However, you cannot alter the color of [Black] or [Registration].)

To change the color of any object, select the object, and then click the color on the palette that you wish to apply.

Changing the Color Palette

You can mix and/or add as many colors as you like to the default color palette, using any of four different color systems: **CMYK**, **PANTONE**, **RGB**, or **HLS**. The last two systems are used only to approximate colors on your screen when the printed colors will be created by mixing colored inks manually at a printshop, rather than from specifications in a PageMaker file. Here is an explanation of each of these methods for handling colors:

- **CMYK** is a model that defines specific colors according to the four process colors: cyan, magenta, yellow, and black.

You can define any other color you want by applying percentages of these colors. CMYK is discussed in Step 20.

- **PANTONE** colors are a system of 700 standard colors developed by Pantone, Inc., and are identified by specific color numbers that are listed in the PANTONE Color Formula Guide.

- **RGB** colors are based on percentages of the three primary colors: red, green, and blue.

- **HLS** colors are defined by percentages of hue, lightness, and saturation.

To define colors by any of these systems, you use the **Edit color** dialog box, shown in Figure 18.1. In this figure you can also see the default **Colors** palette, displayed below the **Styles** palette. This is the procedure for defining a color:

Defining a color

1. Pull down the **Element** menu and select the **Define colors...** command. The **Define colors** dialog box will appear, including a list box that duplicates the items shown on the **Colors** palette. At the right of the dialog box there are the usual **OK** and **Cancel** buttons that let you save or

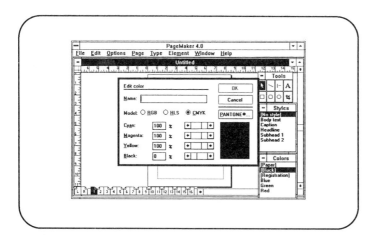

Figure 18.1: The Edit color dialog box shown with the color palette

cancel changes. You will also find these additional buttons: **New**... (for defining or adding a new color to the palette), **Edit**... (for editing a selected color), **Copy**... (for copying colors from another publication), and **Remove** (for deleting a selected color from the palette).

2. To define a new color, click the **New**... button. The **Edit color** dialog box will be displayed as you see it in Figure 18.1, showing by default the color settings that make up black. (The same dialog box is displayed when you select **Edit**..., except that the box will show the current settings for the color you choose.)

3. Click the button for the color system you want to use. (**RGB**, **HLS**, and **CMYK** models are handled in this dialog box; if you click the **Pantone**... button, you'll bring up the special **Pantone Color** dialog box shown in Figure 18.2.)

4. If you're defining a color for a model other than the Pantone system, adjust the color scroll bars until you see the color mixture you want. Alternatively, you can enter a specific percentage for each color, which is often done to match colors to be used by a commercial printshop. Name the color in the text box provided.

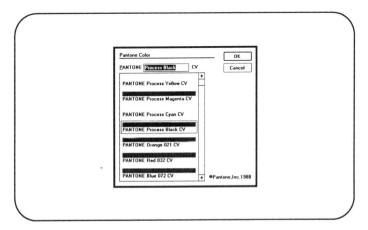

Figure 18.2: The Pantone Color dialog box

5. To select a color in the **Pantone Color** dialog box, scroll the list until you see the color you want, or type its name in the text box. (Note: You don't *define* Pantone colors; the whole point of the Pantone system is that you can select from hundreds of predefined colors, using a numbering system that is recognized in the printing industry the world over.)

6. To return to the **Define colors** dialog box, click **OK** twice for Pantone colors or once for the other systems. At this point you can either define another color or click **OK** again to return to your publication. The colors you've added will now appear on your color palette.

Determining Assigned Colors

Once you have assigned colors to objects in your publication, you may forget exactly which color you have assigned to a text object or drawing—particularly if you have, let us say, five different variations of red on your palette.

You can easily double-check the color assignment. Just do this:

1. Select the object in question.

2. Look at your color palette. The color in use will be highlighted, as shown in Figure 18.3.

3. If you want to change to a different color, scroll the color palette (if necessary) until the color appears, and click to select it.

Figure 18.3: Checking a color assignment

Step 19
Printing Your Publication

15

As you create a publication, PageMaker determines character and line spacing, margins, typefaces, and other page attributes in terms of the currently selected *target printer*. (The target printer is the printer that you have chosen for your output. You can change the printer by pulling down the **File** menu and selecting the **Target Printer...** command.) You may choose to print a draft of the document on another printer. For example, some people who do desktop publishing have only a dot-matrix printer, which they use for proofing purposes; however, they compose every publication for a laser printer because they take the completed Page-Maker files to a printshop, service bureau, or a friend to be printed on a laser. Under these circumstances, it's important to realize that the printed draft will be only a rough approximation of the final product.

Although using different printers for draft and final versions of a publication is an acceptable practice, never change the target printer during the creation of a publication. You may find that several elements of your pages will print incorrectly.

Using Print Dialog Box Options

Although you can print your publications using the standard drivers furnished with Windows, PageMaker adds more sophisticated options than are provided by most other programs. Figure 19.1 shows the PageMaker Print dialog box. In this Step you'll learn the meaning of the basic options in this box that you're likely to need. In Step 20 you'll cover options that relate specifically to commercial and color printing.

You access the **Print dialog** box by pulling down the **File** menu and selecting the **Print...** command. Here is a quick rundown of some of the features in this dialog box:

- **Copies** is where you enter how many copies you want of the publication.

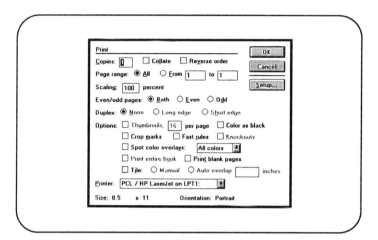

Figure 19.1: The Print dialog box

- **Collate** is the box to check (if you've chosen to make multiple copies) to print each complete copy of the publication in sequence (rather than 3 copies of page 1, then 3 copies of page 2, and so on).

- **Reverse order** causes the last page to be printed first, handy with printers such as the LaserJet Plus and Laser-Writer Plus, which would otherwise print and stack page 2 on top of page 1, rather than behind it.

- **Page range** has the **All** button selected by default; click the **From** button and fill in the starting and ending pages if you wish to print only part of your publication.

- **Scaling** lets you change the default of 100% to any value between 25% and 999%, if you want to enlarge or reduce the printed size of the pages. If you want to print large documents that are too big for your sheets of paper, also select the **Tile** option. Portions of pages will then be printed on separate sheets so you can join them together later. You can overlap these portions automatically by clicking the **Auto overlap** button and entering an overlap amount. As an alternative, you can click **Manual** to set the tiling for each page individually by readjusting the zero point (which is in the upper left corner of the page).

- **Even/odd pages** provides buttons so you can print both even- and odd-numbered pages, only even, or only odd. The purpose of this option is to let you print one side of double-sided pages, and then reload the paper to print the other side. If you have a printer that's capable of printing both sides at once, select **Both**.

- **Duplex** is set by default with the **None** button selected. If you don't have a printer that will print *duplex* (both sides of the paper at once), accept the default. If you do have a duplex printer, click the **Long edge** button if you're printing in the tall orientation (portrait mode) and want the pages of the completed document to turn as if they were pages in a book. Click the **Short edge** button if you want tall pages to turn as if they were pages in a wall calendar. If you're printing in the wide orientation (landscape mode), you would reverse these choices.

- **Thumbnails** is available only if you're using a PostScript printer. When selected, this option prints up to 64 miniature representations of your pages on a sheet of paper so you can analyze the layout of your publication.

- **Color as black** causes black and white printers to print all colored objects as black rather than shades of gray. Selecting this option speeds up the printing of these objects and also prevents light-colored text from being printed as white and therefore becoming invisible.

Other options in the **Print** dialog box that relate to commercial and color printing are explained in Step 20.

When you have finished making any desired changes in this dialog box, click **OK** to start printing.

Step 20
Commercial & Color Printing

This Step will cover special considerations involved in color printing and/or in having your publication printed on equipment not available to your own computer.

Printing to Disk

If you don't have a printer, or you have one that does not provide the quality you want for your publication, you may want to use some other printing facility. You can achieve a resolution of 300 dots per inch with most laser printers. However, a commercial PostScript imagesetter can produce resolution of up to 3,386 dots per inch.

To improve your output, you can print a PageMaker publication to a file and then take it or send it by modem to someone who has the type of printing equipment required.

To print your publication to disk, first you must select Windows options to make this possible. Follow this procedure:

1. If necessary, pull down the **File** menu and select the **Target printer**... command to activate the printer you want to use for the final version of your publication. Click **OK** to save your change and close the **Target printer** dialog box.

2. Click the **Minimize** button to shrink PageMaker to an icon temporarily.

3. Double-click the Windows **Main** icon to open the **Main group** window (unless it's already open).

4. Double-click the **Control Panel** icon to open the **Control Panel** window.

5. Double-click the **Printers** icon. You will now see the **Printers** dialog box.

6. In the **Installed Printers** box, pick your target printer. Then select **Configure.** You'll see the **Configure** dialog box, listing printer ports such as LPT1.

7. From the list of printer ports, select **FILE** as the port.

8. Click **OK** to save your changes and leave the **Configure** dialog box. Click **OK** again to leave the **Printers** dialog box.

9. Double-click the close box in the **Control Panel** and **Main group** windows to return to the desktop.

10. Double-click the PageMaker icon to reactivate the program.

11. Now pull down the PageMaker **File** menu, open the publication you want to print (if it's not open already); then pull down the menu again and select the **Print...** command. The **Print** dialog box will appear.

12. Select any options you need, from among those explained in Step 19 and/or from advanced options explained in the section that follows.

13. From the drop-down **Printer list box,** select the printer you assigned to the **FILE** port.

14. Click **OK.** A Windows **Print To File** dialog box will appear.

15. In this dialog box, type a valid DOS file name for the disk file you want to create of your publication. If you don't include a complete DOS path with the name, the file will be stored in the current directory.

16. Click **OK** to start the print-to-disk procedure.

If you want to take or send the file on disk to a printing facility, obviously it would be handy to print the file directly to a floppy disk. However, your file may be too large to fit on a single floppy. In this case, you can issue a series of print commands to print a few pages of the publication at a time.

Selecting Advanced Printing Options

To print your document in color, or to have it printed by a commercial facility, you may want to change some defaults in the area at the bottom of the **Print** dialog box shown in Figure 20.1.

- **Crop marks,** if checked, will produce marks on a printed copy that will show a printshop the boundaries of your pages and where the paper should be trimmed. However, the marks won't appear unless the page size of your Page-Maker document is at least one-half inch smaller in all dimensions than the paper size of your printer. If you've selected **Spot color overlays** (see the next item), registration marks will be printed on color separations (explained below), along with the name of the color that each separation represents.

- **Spot color overlays,** if checked, will cause overlays (*color separations*) to be printed. A drop-down menu (shown in Figure 20.1) lets you elect to make an overlay for each color in your publication or only a single color you specify. Commercial printing establishments use color separations to produce color printing. These are individual black-and-white pages; each represents the exact areas on the page where a certain color is to be applied. Commercial printers can create any color you want by combining percentages of the four process colors: cyan, magenta, yellow, and black. (See Step 18 for an explanation of the CMYK system.) This method is used to reproduce full-color EPS and TIFF files imported into your PageMaker publications.

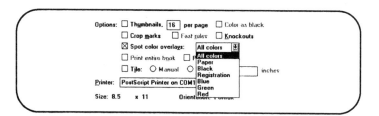

Figure 20.1: Advanced options in the Print dialog box

- **Knockouts**, if checked, will create a blank spot on a bottom overlay at each point where an individual color will be applied from another overlay. Select this option only if you've also selected **Spot color overlays.** A commercial printshop may prefer to make these knockouts manually for you; be sure to ask. A typical knockout might create a "hole" in a photograph where a colored title would be superimposed from its own overlay.

Index

A

Actual size option, 48
Adobe Type Manager (ATM), 9, 16–20, 55
AGFA Compugraphic, Type Director, 20
Aldus group icon, 22
Aldus Setup window, 4–5
alignment (justification), 33
alignment of objects, 27
alphabetic characters, for page numbers, 61
angle brackets, for tags, 68
As New Story option, 67
attributes of fonts, 32
 changing, 82, 87–88
 searching for, 86–87
AUTOEXEC.BAT file, 7, 14
Autoflow command, 65–66, 68
autoleading, 103

B

background for text, 36–37
baseline, ruler guide for, 57
bitmapped fonts, 11, 13
Bitstream, 20
Book command, 27
Bring to front command, 37

C

Cascade command, 28
center alignment tabs, 95
Change command, 87–88
characters, spacing between, 99–100
ciceros, as measurement system, 52
circles, 39
Clear command, 82
CMYK color system, 116–117
Collate option, 122
color, 115–119
 checking assignment of, 119
 defining, 117–119
Color as black printing, 123
color palette, 115–119
color separations, 116, 127
Column-break icon, 74
columns, 58–60
 changing width of, 59
 full justification of, 101
composite number system, 61, 63
CONFIG.SYS file, 7
Control Panel
 for Adobe Type Manager, 18–19
 for Windows, 10
Convert quotes option, 67

vertical ruler, measurement
system for, 53

W

Wide orientation, 23–24
widow control, 54
Window menu, 28, 115–116
Windows
  Control Panel, 10
  opening, 21
  for printing to disk, 125

Program Manager, 2
windows, maximizing, 80
Windows clipboard, 41, 68–69
windowshades, 35, 69
Word space, 101
word wrap, 28
word-processing. *See* story view
Wrap-all-sides icon,74–75

Z

zero point, 55–57
zooming in, 47

Selections from The SYBEX Library

DESKTOP PUBLISHING

The ABC's of the New Print Shop
Vivian Dubrovin
340pp. Ref. 640-4
This beginner's guide stresses fun, practicality and original ideas. Hands-on tutorials show how to create greeting cards, invitations, signs, flyers, letterheads, banners, and calendars.

The ABC's of Ventura
Robert Cowart
Steve Cummings
390pp. Ref. 537-9
Created especially for new desktop publishers, this is an easy introduction to a complex program. Cowart provides details on using the mouse, the Ventura side bar, and page layout, with careful explanations of publishing terminology. The new Ventura menus are all carefully explained. For Version 2.

Mastering CorelDRAW!
Steve Rimmer
403pp. Ref. 685-5
This four-color tutorial and user's guide covers drawing and tracing, text and special effects, file interchange, and adding new fonts. With in-depth treatment of design principles. For version 1.1.

Mastering PageMaker on the IBM PC (Second Edition)
Antonia Stacy Jolles
384pp. Ref. 521-2
A guide to every aspect of desktop publishing with PageMaker: the vocabulary and basics of page design, layout, graphics and typography, plus instructions for creating finished typeset publications of all kinds.

Mastering Ventura for Windows (For Version 3.0)
Rick Altman
600pp, Ref. 758-4
This engaging, hands-on treatment is for the desktop publisher learning and using the Windows edition of Ventura. It covers everything from working with the Windows interface, to designing and printing sophisticated publications using Ventura's most advanced features. Understand and work with frames, graphics, fonts, tables and columns, and much more.

Mastering Ventura 3.0 Gem Edition
Matthew Holtz
650pp, Ref. 703-7
The complete hands-on guide to desktop publishing with Xerox Ventura Publisher— now in an up-to-date new edition featuring Ventura version 3.0, with the GEM windowing environment. Tutorials cover every aspect of the software, with examples ranging from correspondence and press releases, to newsletters, technical documents, and more.

Understanding PFS: First Publisher
Gerry Litton
310pp. Ref. 616-2
This complete guide takes users from the basics all the way through the most complex features available. Discusses working with text and graphics, columns, clip art, and add-on software enhancements. Many page layout suggestions are introduced. Includes Fast Track speed notes.

Understanding PostScript Programming (Second Edition)
David A. Holzgang
472pp. Ref. 566-2
In-depth treatment of PostScript for programmers and advanced users working

on custom desktop publishing tasks. Hands-on development of programs for font creation, integrating graphics, printer implementations and more.

Ventura Instant Reference
SYBEX Prompter Series
Matthew Holtz
320pp. Ref. 544-1, 4 ¾" × 8"
This compact volume offers easy access to the complex details of Ventura modes and options, commands, side-bars, file management, output device configuration, and control. Written for versions through Ventura 2, it also includes standard procedures for project and job control.

Ventura Power Tools
Rick Altman
318pp. Ref. 592-1
Renowned Ventura expert, Rick Altman, presents strategies and techniques for the most efficient use of Ventura Publisher 2. This includes a power disk with DOS utilities which is specially designed for optimizing Ventura use. Learn how to soup up Ventura, edit CHP files, avoid design tragedies, handle very large documents, and improve form.

Your HP LaserJet Handbook
Alan R. Neibauer
564pp. Ref. 618-9
Get the most from your printer with this step-by-step instruction book for using LaserJet text and graphics features such as cartridge and soft fonts, type selection, memory and processor enhancements, PCL programming, and PostScript solutions. This hands-on guide provides specific instructions for working with a variety of software.

CAD

The ABC's of AutoCAD
(Second Edition)
Alan R. Miller
375pp. Ref. 584-0
This brief but effective introduction to AutoCAD quickly gets users drafting and designing with this complex CADD package. The essential operations and capabilities of AutoCAD are neatly detailed, using a proven, step-by-step method that is tailored to the results-oriented beginner.

The ABC's of AutoLISP
George Omura
300pp. Ref. 620-0
This book is for users who want to unleash the full power of AutoCAD through the AutoLISP programming language. In non-technical terms, the reader is shown how to store point locations, create new commands, and manipulate coordinates and text. Packed with tips on common coding errors.

The ABC's of Generic CADD
Alan R. Miller
278pp. Ref. 608-1
This outstanding guide to computer-aided design and drafting with Generic CADD assumes no previous experience with computers or CADD. This book will have users doing useful CADD work in record time, including basic drawing with the keyboard or a mouse, erasing and unerasing, making a copy of drawings on your printer, adding text and organizing your drawings using layers.

Advanced Techniques
in AutoCAD
(Second Edition)
Robert M. Thomas
425pp. Ref. 593-X
Develop custom applications using screen menus, command macros, and AutoLISP programming—no prior programming experience required. Topics include customizing the AutoCAD environment, advanced data extraction techniques, and much more.

AutoCAD Desktop Companion
SYBEX Ready Reference Series
Robert M. Thomas
1094pp. Ref. 590-5
This is a complete reference work covering all the features, commands, and user options available under AutoCAD Release 10, including drawing basic and complex entities, editing, displaying, printing, plotting, and customizing draw-

ings, manipulating the drawing database, and AutoLISP programming. Through Release 10.

AutoCAD Instant Reference
SYBEX Prompter Series
George Omura
390pp. Ref. 548-4, 4 ¾" × 8"
This pocket-sized reference is a quick guide to all AutoCAD features. Designed for easy use, all commands are organized with exact syntax, a brief description, options, tips, and references. Through Release 10.

Mastering AutoCAD Release 11
George Omura
1150pp, Ref. 716-9
Even if you're just beginning, this comprehensive guide will help you to become an AutoCAD expert. Create your first drawing, then learn to use dimensions, enter pre-existing drawings, use advanced 3-D features, and more. Suitable for experienced users, too—includes tips and tricks you won't find elsewhere.

Mastering VersaCAD
David Bassett-Parkins
450pp. Ref. 617-0
For every level of VCAD user, this comprehensive tutorial treats each phase of project design including drawing, modifying, grouping, and filing. The reader will also learn VCAD project management and many tips, tricks, and shortcuts. Version 5.4.

WORD PROCESSING

The ABC's of Microsoft Word (Third Edition)
Alan R. Neibauer
461pp. Ref. 604-9
This is for the novice WORD user who wants to begin producing documents in the shortest time possible. Each chapter has short, easy-to-follow lessons for both keyboard and mouse, including all the basic editing, formatting and printing functions. Version 5.0.

The ABC's of WordPerfect
Alan R. Neibauer
239pp. Ref. 425-9
This basic introduction to WordPefect consists of short, step-by-step lessons— for new users who want to get going fast. Topics range from simple editing and formatting, to merging, sorting, macros, and more. Includes version 4.2

The ABC's of WordPerfect 5
Alan R. Neibauer
283pp. Ref. 504-2
This introduction explains the basics of desktop publishing with WordPerfect 5: editing, layout, formatting, printing, sorting, merging, and more. Readers are shown how to use WordPerfect 5's new features to produce great-looking reports.

The ABC's of WordPerfect 5.1
Alan R. Neibauer
352pp. Ref. 672-3
Neibauer's delightful writing style makes this clear tutorial an especially effective learning tool. Learn all about 5.1's new drop-down menus and mouse capabilities that reduce the tedious memorization of function keys.

The Complete Guide to MultiMate
Carol Holcomb Dreger
208pp. Ref. 229-9
This step-by-step tutorial is also an excellent reference guide to MultiMate features and uses. Topics include search/replace, library and merge functions, repagination, document defaults and more.

Encyclopedia WordPerfect 5.1
Greg Harvey
Kay Yarborough Nelson
1100pp. Ref. 676-6
This comprehensive, up-to-date WordPerfect reference is a must for beginning and experienced users alike. With complete, easy-to-find information on every

WordPerfect feature and command—and it's organized by practical functions, with business users in mind.

Introduction to WordStar
Arthur Naiman
208pp. Ref. 134-9

This all time bestseller is an engaging first-time introduction to word processing as well as a complete guide to using WordStar—from basic editing to blocks, global searches, formatting, dot commands, SpellStar and MailMerge. Through Version 3.3.

Mastering Microsoft Word on the IBM PC (Fourth Edition)
Matthew Holtz
680pp. Ref. 597-2

This comprehensive, step-by-step guide details all the new desktop publishing developments in this versatile word processor, including details on editing, formatting, printing, and laser printing. Holtz uses sample business documents to demonstrate the use of different fonts, graphics, and complex documents. Includes Fast Track speed notes. For Versions 4 and 5.

Mastering MultiMate Advantage II
Charles Ackerman
407pp. Ref. 482-8

This comprehensive tutorial covers all the capabilities of MultiMate, and highlights the differences between MultiMate Advantage II and previous versions—in pathway support, sorting, math, DOS access, using dBASE III, and more. With many practical examples, and a chapter on the On-File database.

Mastering WordPerfect
Susan Baake Kelly
435pp. Ref. 332-5

Step-by-step training from startup to mastery, featuring practical uses (form letters, newsletters and more), plus advanced topics such as document security and

macro creation, sorting and columnar math. Through Version 4.2.

Mastering WordPerfect 5
Susan Baake Kelly
709pp. Ref. 500-X

The revised and expanded version of this definitive guide is now on WordPerfect 5 and covers wordprocessing and basic desktop publishing. As more than 200,000 readers of the original edition can attest, no tutorial approaches it for clarity and depth of treatment. Sorting, line drawing, and laser printing included.

Mastering WordPerfect 5.1
Alan Simpson
1050pp. Ref. 670-7

The ultimate guide for the WordPerfect user. Alan Simpson, the "master communicator," puts you in charge of the latest features of 5.1: new dropdown menus and mouse capabilities, along with the desktop publishing, macro programming, and file conversion functions that have made WordPerfect the most popular word processing program on the market.

Mastering WordStar Release 5.5
Greg Harvey
David J. Clark
450pp. Ref. 491-7

This book is the ultimate reference book for the newest version of WordStar. Readers may use Mastering to look up any word processing function, including the new Version 5 and 5.5 features and enhancements, and find detailed instructions for fundamental to advanced operations.

Microsoft Word Instant Reference for the IBM PC
Matthew Holtz
266pp. Ref. 692-8

Turn here for fast, easy access to concise information on every command and feature of Microsoft Word version 5.0—for editing, formatting, merging, style sheets, macros, and more. With exact keystroke sequences, discussion of command options, and commonly-performed tasks.

Practical WordStar Uses
Julie Anne Arca
303pp. Ref. 107-1
A hands-on guide to WordStar and MailMerge applications, with solutions to comon problems and "recipes" for day-to-day tasks. Formatting, merge-printing and much more; plus a quick-reference command chart and notes on CP/M and PC-DOS. For Version 3.3.

Understanding Professional Write
Gerry Litton
400pp. Ref. 656-1
A complete guide to Professional Write that takes you from creating your first simple document, into a detailed description of all major aspects of the software. Special features place an emphasis on the use of different typestyles to create attractive documents as well as potential problems and suggestions on how to get around them.

Understanding WordStar 2000
David Kolodney
Thomas Blackadar
275pp. Ref. 554-9
This engaging, fast-paced series of tutorials covers everything from moving the cursor to print enhancements, format files, key glossaries, windows and MailMerge. With practical examples, and notes for former WordStar users.

Visual Guide to WordPerfect
Jeff Woodward
457pp. Ref. 591-3
This is a visual hands-on guide which is ideal for brand new users as the book shows each activity keystroke-by-keystroke. Clear illustrations of computer screen menus are included at every stage. Covers basic editing, formatting lines, paragraphs, and pages, using the block feature, footnotes, search and replace, and more. Through Version 5.

WordPerfect 5 Desktop Companion
SYBEX Ready Reference Series
Greg Harvey
Kay Yarborough Nelson
1006pp. Ref. 522-0
Desktop publishing features have been added to this compact encyclopedia. This title offers more detailed, cross-referenced entries on every software feature including page formatting and layout, laser printing and word processing macros. New users of WordPerfect, and those new to Version 5 and desktop publishing will find this easy to use for on-the-job help.

WordPerfect 5 Instant Reference
SYBEX Prompter Series
Greg Harvey
Kay Yarborough Nelson
316pp. Ref. 535-2, 4 3/4" × 8"
This pocket-sized reference has all the program commands for the powerful WordPerfect 5 organized alphabetically for quick access. Each command entry has the exact key sequence, any reveal codes, a list of available options, and option-by-option discussions.

WordPerfect 5.1 Instant Reference
Greg Harvey
Kay Yarborough Nelson
252pp. Ref. 674-X
Instant access to all features and commands of WordPerfect 5.0 and 5.1, highlighting the newest software features. Complete, alphabetical entries provide exact key sequences, codes and options, and step-by-step instructions for many important tasks.

WordPerfect 5.1 Macro Handbook
Kay Yarborough Nelson
532pp, Ref. 687-1
Help yourself to over 150 ready-made macros for WordPerfect versions 5.0 and 5.1. This complete tutorial guide to creating and using work-saving macros is a

must for every serious WordPerfect user. Hands-on lessons show you exactly how to record and use your first simple macros—then build to sophisticated skills.

WordPerfect 5.1 Tips and Tricks (Fourth Edition)
Alan R. Neibauer
675pp. Ref. 681-2
This new edition is a real timesaver. For on-the-job guidance and creative new uses, this title covers all versions of WordPerfect up to and including 5.1—streamlining documents, automating with macros, new print enhancements, and more.

WordStar Instant Reference SYBEX Prompter Series
David J. Clark
314pp. Ref. 543-3, 4 ¾" × 8"
This quick reference provides reminders on the use of the editing, formatting, mailmerge, and document processing commands available through WordStar 4 and 5. Operations are organized alphabetically for easy access. The text includes a survey of the menu system and instructions for installing and customizing WordStar.

OPERATING SYSTEMS

The ABC's of DOS 4
Alan R. Miller
275pp. Ref. 583-2
This step-by-step introduction to using DOS 4 is written especially for beginners. Filled with simple examples, *The ABC's of DOS 4* covers the basics of hardware, software, disks, the system editor EDLIN, DOS commands, and more.

ABC's of MS-DOS (Second Edition)
Alan R. Miller
233pp. Ref. 493-3
This handy guide to MS-DOS is all many PC users need to manage their computer files, organize floppy and hard disks, use

EDLIN, and keep their computers organized. Additional information is given about utilities like Sidekick, and there is a DOS command and program summary. The second edition is fully updated for Version 3.3.

DOS Assembly Language Programming
Alan R. Miller
365pp. 487-9
This book covers PC-DOS through 3.3, and gives clear explanations of how to assemble, link, and debug 8086, 8088, 80286, and 80386 programs. The example assembly language routines are valuable for students and programmers alike.

DOS Instant Reference SYBEX Prompter Series
Greg Harvey
Kay Yarborough Nelson
220pp. Ref. 477-1, 4 ¾" × 8"
A complete fingertip reference for fast, easy on-line help:command summaries, syntax, usage and error messages. Organized by function—system commands, file commands, disk management, directories, batch files, I/O, networking, programming, and more. Through Version 3.3.

Encyclopedia DOS
Judd Robbins
1030pp. Ref. 699-5
A comprehensive reference and user's guide to all versions of DOS through 4.0. Offers complete information on every DOS command, with all possible switches and parameters—plus examples of effective usage. An invaluable tool.

Essential OS/2 (Second Edition)
Judd Robbins
445pp. Ref. 609-X
Written by an OS/2 expert, this is the guide to the powerful new resources of the OS/2 operating system standard edition 1.1 with presentation manager. Robbins introduces the standard edition, and details multitasking under OS/2, and the

range of commands for installing, starting up, configuring, and running applications. For Version 1.1 Standard Edition.

Essential PC-DOS
(Second Edition)
Myril Clement Shaw
Susan Soltis Shaw
332pp. Ref. 413-5
An authoritative guide to PC-DOS, including version 3.2. Designed to make experts out of beginners, it explores everything from disk management to batch file programming. Includes an 85-page command summary. Through Version 3.2.

Graphics Programming
Under Windows
Brian Myers
Chris Doner
646pp. Ref. 448-8
Straightforward discussion, abundant examples, and a concise reference guide to graphics commands make this book a must for Windows programmers. Topics range from how Windows works to programming for business, animation, CAD, and desktop publishing. For Version 2.

Hard Disk Instant Reference
SYBEX Prompter Series
Judd Robbins
256pp. Ref. 587-5, 4 ¾" × 8"
Compact yet comprehensive, this pocket-sized reference presents the essential information on DOS commands used in managing directories and files, and in optimizing disk configuration. Includes a survey of third-party utility capabilities. Through DOS 4.0.

Inside DOS: A Programmer's
Guide
Michael J. Young
490pp. Ref. 710-X
A collection of practical techniques (with source code listings) designed to help you take advantage of the rich resources intrinsic to MS-DOS machines. Designed for the experienced programmer with a basic understanding of C and 8086 assembly language, and DOS fundamentals.

Mastering DOS
(Second Edition)
Judd Robbins
722pp. Ref. 555-7
"The most useful DOS book." This seven-part, in-depth tutorial addresses the needs of users at all levels. Topics range from running applications, to managing files and directories, configuring the system, batch file programming, and techniques for system developers. Through Version 4.

MS-DOS Power User's Guide,
Volume I
(Second Edition)
Jonathan Kamin
482pp. Ref. 473-9
A fully revised, expanded edition of our best-selling guide to high-performance DOS techniques and utilities—with details on Version 3.3. Configuration, I/O, directory structures, hard disks, RAM disks, batch file programming, the ANSI.SYS device driver, more. Through Version 3.3.

Understanding DOS 3.3
Judd Robbins
678pp. Ref. 648-0
This best selling, in-depth tutorial addresses the needs of users at all levels with many examples and hands-on exercises. Robbins discusses the fundamentals of DOS, then covers manipulating files and directories, using the DOS editor, printing, communicating, and finishes with a full section on batch files.

Understanding Hard Disk
Management on the PC
Jonathan Kamin
500pp. Ref. 561-1
This title is a key productivity tool for all hard disk users who want efficient, error-free file management and organization. Includes details on the best ways to conserve hard disk space when using several memory-guzzling programs. Through DOS 4.

Up & Running with Your Hard Disk
Klaus M Rubsam
140pp. Ref. 666-9

A far-sighted, compact introduction to hard disk installation and basic DOS use. Perfect for PC users who want the practical essentials in the shortest possible time. In 20 basic steps, learn to choose your hard disk, work with accessories, back up data, use DOS utilities to save time, and more.

Up & Running with Windows 286/386
Gabriele Wentges
132pp. Ref. 691-X

This handy 20-step overview gives PC users all the essentials of using Windows—whether for evaluating the software, or getting a fast start. Each self-contained lesson takes just 15 minutes to one hour to complete.

UTILITIES

Mastering the Norton Utilities 5
Peter Dyson
400pp, Ref. 725-8

This complete guide to installing and using the Norton Utilities 5 is a must for beginning and experienced users alike. It offers a clear, detailed description of each utility, with options, uses and examples—so users can quickly identify the programs they need and put Norton right to work. Includes valuable coverage of the newest Norton enhancements.

Mastering PC Tools Deluxe 6
For Versions 5.5 and 6.0
425pp, Ref. 700-2

An up-to-date guide to the lifesaving utilities in PC Tools Deluxe version 6.0 from installation, to high-speed back-ups, data recovery, file encryption, desktop applications, and more. Includes detailed background on DOS and hardware such as floppies, hard disks, modems and fax cards.

Mastering SideKick Plus
Gene Weisskopf
394pp. Ref. 558-1

Employ all of Sidekick's powerful and expanded features with this hands-on guide to the popular utility. Features include comprehensive and detailed coverage of time management, note taking, outlining, auto dialing, DOS file management, math, and copy-and-paste functions.

Up & Running with Norton Utilities
Rainer Bartel
140pp. Ref. 659-6

Get up and running in the shortest possible time in just 20 lessons or "steps." Learn to restore disks and files, use UnErase, edit your floppy disks, retrieve lost data and more. Or use the book to evaluate the software before you purchase. Through Version 4.2.

Up & Running with PC Tools Deluxe 6
Thomas Holste
180pp. Ref.678-2

Learn to use this software program in just 20 basic steps. Readers get a quick, inexpensive introduction to using the Tools for disaster recovery, disk and file management, and more.

COMMUNICATIONS

Mastering Crosstalk XVI (Second Edition)
Peter W. Gofton
225pp. Ref. 642-1

Introducing the communications program Crosstalk XVI for the IBM PC. As well as providing extensive examples of command and script files for programming Crosstalk, this book includes a detailed description of how to use the program's more advanced features, such as windows, talking to mini or mainframe, customizing the keyboard and answering calls and background mode.

Mastering PROCOMM PLUS
Bob Campbell
400pp. Ref. 657-X
Learn all about communications and information retrieval as you master and use PROCOMM PLUS. Topics include choosing and using a modem; automatic dialing; using on-line services (featuring CompuServe) and more. Through Version 1.1b; also covers PROCOMM, the "shareware" version.

Mastering Serial Communications
Peter W. Gofton
289pp. Ref. 180-2
The software side of communications, with details on the IBM PC's serial programming, the XMODEM and Kermit protocols, non-ASCII data transfer, interrupt-level programming and more. Sample programs in C, assembly language and BASIC.

APPLE/MACINTOSH

ABC's of Excel on the Macintosh (Second Edition)
Douglas Hergert
334pp. Ref. 634-0
Newly updated to include version 2.2, this tutorial offers a quick way for beginners to get started doing useful work with Excel. Readers build practical examples for accounting, management, and home/office applications, as they learn to create worksheets, charts, databases, macros, and more.

Desktop Publishing with Microsoft Word on the Macintosh (Second Edition)
Tim Erickson
William Finzer
525pp. Ref. 601-4
The authors have woven a murder mystery through the text, using the sample publications as clues. Explanations of page layout, headings, fonts and styles, columnar text, and graphics are interwoven within the mystery theme of this exciting teaching method. For Version 4.0.

Encyclopedia Macintosh
Craig Danuloff
Deke McClelland
650pp. Ref. 628-6
Just what every Mac user needs—a complete reference to Macintosh concepts and tips on system software, hardware, applications, and troubleshooting. Instead of chapters, each section is presented in A-Z format with user-friendly icons leading the way.

Mastering Adobe Illustrator
David A. Holzgang
330pp. Ref. 463-1
This text provides a complete introduction to Adobe Illustrator, bringing new sophistication to artists using computer-aided graphics and page design technology. Includes a look at PostScript, the page composition language used by Illustrator.

Mastering AppleWorks (Second Edition)
Elna Tymes
479pp. Ref. 398-8
New chapters on business applications, data sharing DIF and Applesoft BASIC make this practical, in-depth tutorial even better. Full details on AppleWorks desktop, word processing, spreadsheet and database functions.

Mastering Excel on the Macintosh (Third Edition)
Carl Townsend
656pp. Ref. 622-7
This highly acclaimed tutorial has been updated for the latest version of Excel. Full of extensive examples, tips, application templates, and illustrations. This book makes a great reference for using worksheets, databases, graphics, charts, macros, and tables. For Version 2.2.

Mastering Microsoft Word on the Macintosh
Michael J. Young
447pp. Ref. 541-7
This comprehensive, step-by-step guide shows the reader through WORD's extensive capabilities, from basic editing to custom formats and desktop publishing. Keyboard and mouse instructions and practice exercises are included. For Release 4.0.

Mastering Powerpoint
Karen L. McGraw, Ph.D.
425pp. Ref. 646-4
The complete guide to creating high-quality graphic presentations using PowerPoint 2.01 on the Macintosh—offering detailed, step-by-step coverage of everything from starting up the software to fine-tuning your slide shows for maximum effect.

Mastering Ready, Set, Go!
David A. Kater
482pp. Ref. 536-0
This hands-on introduction to the popular desktop publishing package for the Macintosh allows readers to produce professional-looking reports, brochures, and flyers. Written for Version 4, this title has been endorsed by Letraset, the Ready, Set, Go! software publisher.

Understanding Hard Disk Management on the Macintosh
J. Russell Roberts
334pp. Ref. 579-4
This is the most comprehensive and accessible guide to hard disk usage for all Macintosh users. Complete coverage includes SCSI and serial drives and ports, formatting, file fragmentation, backups, networks, and a helpful diagnostic appendix.

Understanding HyperCard (Second Edition)
Greg Harvey
654pp. Ref. 607-3
For Mac users who want clear-cut steps to quick mastery of HyperCard, this thorough tutorial introduces HyperCard from the Browsing/Typing and Authoring/Painting levels all the way to Scripting with HyperTalk, the HyperCard programming language. No prior programming experience needed. For Version 1.2.

Using the Macintosh Toolbox with C (Second Edition)
Fred A. Huxham
David Burnard
Jim Takatsuka
525pp. Ref. 572-7
Learn to program with the latest versions of Macintosh Toolbox using this clear and succinct introduction. This popular title has been revised and expanded to include dozens of new programming examples for windows, menus, controls, alert boxes, and disk I/O. Includes hierarchical file system, Lightspeed C, Resource files, and R Maker.

NETWORKS

The ABC's of Local Area Networks
Michael Dortch
212pp. Ref. 664-2
This jargon-free introduction to LANs is for current and prospective users who see general information, comparative options, a look at the future, and tips for effective LANs use today. With comparisons of Token-Ring, PC Network, Novell, and others.

The ABC's of Novell Netware
Jeff Woodward
282pp. Ref. 614-6
For users who are new to PC's or networks, this entry-level tutorial outlines each basic element and operation of Novell. The ABC's introduces computer hardware and software, DOS, network organization and security, and printing and communicating over the netware system.

Mastering Novell Netware
Cheryl C. Currid
Craig A. Gillett
500pp. Ref. 630-8
This book is a thorough guide for System Administrators to installing and operating a microcomputer network using Novell Netware. Mastering covers actually setting up a network from start to finish, design, administration, maintenance, and troubleshooting.

DATABASES

The ABC's of dBASE III PLUS
Robert Cowart
264pp. Ref. 379-1
The most efficient way to get beginners up and running with dBASE. Every 'how' and 'why' of database management is demonstrated through tutorials and practical dBASE III PLUS applications.

The ABC's of dBASE IV 1.1
Robert Cowart
350pp, Ref. 632-4
The latest version of dBASE IV is featured in this hands-on introduction. It assumes no previous experience with computers or database management, and uses easy-to-follow lessons to introduce the concepts, build basic skills, and set up some practical applications. Includes report writing and Query by Example.

The ABC's of Paradox 3.5 (Second Edition)
Charles Siegel
334pp, Ref. 785-1
This easy-to-follow, hands-on tutorial is a must for beginning users of Paradox 3.0 and 3.5. Even if you've never used a computer before, you'll be doing useful work in just a few short lessons. A clear introduction to database management and valuable business examples make this a "right-to-work" guide for the practical-minded.

Advanced Techniques in dBASE III PLUS
Alan Simpson
454pp. Ref. 369-4
A full course in database design and structured programming, with routines for inventory control, accounts receivable, system management, and integrated databases.

dBASE Instant Reference
SYBEX Prompter Series
Alan Simpson
471pp. Ref. 484-4; 4 ¾" × 8"
Comprehensive information at a glance: a brief explanation of syntax and usage for every dBASE command, with step-by-step instructions and exact keystroke sequences. Commands are grouped by function in twenty precise categories.

dBASE III PLUS Programmer's Reference Guide
SYBEX Ready Reference Series
Alan Simpson
1056pp. Ref. 508-5
Programmers will save untold hours and effort using this comprehensive, well-organized dBASE encyclopedia. Complete technical details on commands and functions, plus scores of often-needed algorithms.

dBASE IV 1.1 Programmer's Instant Reference (Second Edition)
Alan Simpson
555pp, Ref. 764-9
Enjoy fast, easy access to information often hidden in cumbersome documentation. This handy pocket-sized reference presents information on each command and function in the dBASE IV programming language. Commands are grouped according to their purpose, so readers can locate the correct command for any task—quickly and easily.

PageMaker Menus

Here are PageMaker's **Type, Element, Window,** and **Help** pull- down menus.

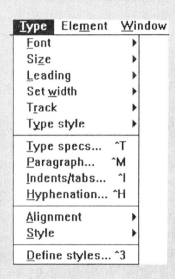

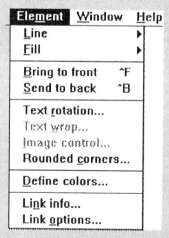